What Your Colleagues Are Saying

This is a book that teachers, coaches, and administrators need to
responsive teaching is the best teaching, and it is also quite difficult to do well. Melanie
and Kelsey do a beautiful job in offering classroom teachers thoughtful, practical ways
to make their writing planning and instruction more responsive. I can't wait to use this
book in my classroom and share it with colleagues!

—Christina Nosek

Classroom teacher and coauthor of

To Know and Nurture a Reader: Conferring With Confidence and Joy

Melanie Meehan and Kelsey Sorum's new text is bursting with fresh ideas that honor
students, build connections, and create a clear vision for community-minded learning.
The Responsive Writing Teacher is not only visually stunning but also smart, practical,
and oh so needed! Meehan and Sorum help teachers shift from relying solely on curriculum guides to also using what they know about students (academically, linguistically,
culturally, and socially-emotionally) to contemplate, plan, and implement high-quality instruction that makes sense for current learners. Throughout the text, there is
a strong emphasis on intentional and habitual information collecting and efficient
methods for turning these curated noticings into responsive teaching. The abundance
of included tools support readers in implementing instruction that sees, respects, and
builds on all aspects of classroom learners' identities. I especially appreciate the combination of the why, what, how, when, and where behind each brilliant tool Meehan
and Sorum include. Further, the recurring Tips for Tomorrow feature crystalizes how
to implement each shared idea immediately. Without a doubt, this is THE book that
needs to be in the hands of every educator right now.

—Pamela Koutrakos

Author of *Word Study That Sticks* and

The Word Study That Sticks Companion

This thoughtful and thorough resource has so many actionable ideas and tools I'm
surprised they're not spilling out of the book! Melanie and Kelsey share their wisdom
honed from deep study as they mindfully weave academic, linguistic, cultural, and
social-emotional responsiveness into the components of writing instruction. With
these two writing teachers by your side, you'll transform your teaching space into one
where ALL writers are honored, supported, and celebrated.

—Maria Walther

Traveling teacher, literacy consultant, and author of

The Ramped-Up Read Aloud: What to Notice as You Turn the Page, and coauthor of

The Literacy Workshop: Where Reading and Writing Converge

If you are a teacher who is curious about who your students are, what they bring as strengths, and what specific needs they have, Melanie and Kelsey will show you how to use a framework of inquiry to grow writers by being responsive to their abilities, identities, experiences, and needs. They truly help us keep our focus on the whole child as a writer, not just the writing.

—Paula Bourque

Author of *Close Writing: Developing Purposeful Writers in Grades 2–6*
and *SPARK! Quick Writes to Kindle Hearts and Minds in Elementary Classrooms*

I believe *The Responsive Writing Teacher, Grades K–5* is a book for our times because it helps teachers get to know their students—whether they're teaching face-to-face or remotely. In this book, Melanie and Kelsey help educators rethink the ways things have always been done so all young writers' needs can be met while teaching them how to become more independent. *The Responsive Writing Teacher* is an enduring gift for writing teachers who strive to be academically, culturally, linguistically, and socially-emotionally responsive to students.

—Stacey Shubitz

Literacy consultant, chief of operations for the *Two Writing Teachers* blog, and author of *Welcome to Writing Workshop: Engaging Today's Students With a Model That Works*

The Responsive Writing Teacher, Grades K–5 is comprehensive without being overwhelming. If you want to push your writing instruction to the next level—and at the same time serve the whole child—explore this book!

—Lynn Angus Ramos

K–12 English language arts coordinator,
DeKalb County School District, GA

The Responsive Writing Teacher

Grades K–5

From Melanie: *Wendy, this one is for you. You have pushed my thinking and made me a better educator and person more than you know.*

From Kelsey: *For my big sister, Jana. You gave me courage to fly.*

The Responsive Writing Teacher

Grades K–5

A Hands-On Guide to Child-Centered, Equitable Instruction

Melanie Meehan

Kelsey Sorum

Foreword by Cornelius Minor

CORWIN Literacy

For information:

Corwin
A SAGE Company
2455 Teller Road
Thousand Oaks, California 91320
(800) 233–9936
www.corwin.com

SAGE Publications Ltd.
1 Oliver's Yard
55 City Road
London EC1Y 1SP
United Kingdom

SAGE Publications India Pvt. Ltd.
B 1/I 1 Mohan Cooperative In-
dustrial Area
Mathura Road, New Delhi 110 044
India

SAGE Publications Asia-Pacific Pte. Ltd.
18 Cross Street #10–10/11/12
China Square Central
Singapore 048423

Acquisitions Editor: Tori Bachman
Editorial Development Manager:
    Julie Nemer
*Associate Content Development
    Manager:* Sharon Wu
Project Editor: Amy Schroller
Copy Editor: Megan Markanich
Typesetter: Integra
Proofreader: Lawrence W. Baker
Indexer: Integra
Cover Designer: Gail Buschman
Marketing Manager: Deena Meyer

Printed in the United States of America

Library of Congress Cataloging-in-Publication Data

Names: Meehan, Melanie, author. | Sorum, Kelsey, author.
Title: The responsive writing teacher, grades K-5 : A hands-on guide to
    child-centered, equitable instruction / Melanie Meehan, Kelsey Sorum.
Description: Thousand Oaks, California : Corwin, [2021] | Includes
    bibliographical references and index. | Summary: "This book guides
    teachers through key principles of writing instruction for K–5 students,
    with careful consideration of four domains of responsivity: cognitive,
    linguistic, cultural, and emotional. Many planning, assessment, and
    instructional tools are provided for immediate use or customization"–
    Provided by publisher.
Identifiers: LCCN 2020042261 | ISBN 9781071840641 (paperback) | ISBN
    9781071841310 (ebook) | ISBN 9781071841297 (ebook) | ISBN 9781071840894
    (adobe pdf)
Subjects: LCSH: English language–Composition and exercises–Study and
    teaching (Elementary)
Classification: LCC LB1576 .M4345 2021 | DDC 372.6–dc23
LC record available at https://lccn.loc.gov/2020042261

This book is printed on acid-free paper.

21 22 23 24 25 10 9 8 7 6 5 4 3 2 1

Contents

Visit the companion website at
resources.corwin.com/responsivewritingteacher
for downloadable resources related to this book.

Academic Responsiveness	Linguistic Responsiveness	Cultural Responsiveness	Social-Emotional Responsiveness
Ensuring new skills and content match students' abilities and goals	*Ensuring language(s) used in instruction and in the classroom environment are accessible and inclusive of home language(s)*	*Ensuring a diverse representation of authorship and within the content of texts*	*Ensuring a safe and supportive environment for taking risks and overcoming challenges in the writing process*

Chapter 1 Collect information about. . .

Academic Responsiveness	Linguistic Responsiveness	Cultural Responsiveness	Social-Emotional Responsiveness
Students' proficiency with content-related skills Writing-related behaviors as students engage in a writing process	Students' home language(s), speaking and processing skills, language use, and vocabulary development	The cultural and social identities of students	Student interests within and outside of school The social-emotional tendencies of students in relation to writing

Chapter 2 Plan instruction that has. . .

Academic Responsiveness	Linguistic Responsiveness	Cultural Responsiveness	Social-Emotional Responsiveness
Multiple entry points for students to access instruction and develop skills Differentiated systems and structures for students to access instruction and practice independently	Supports to help students understand, communicate, and develop content-specific language and vocabulary Supports for students who are developing expressive and receptive language	Connections, contexts, and content that is reflective of diverse communities	Writing experiences that are meaningful and align with student interests Safe and supportive opportunities for students to take risks and work collaboratively

Chapter 3 Co-create charts that. . .

Academic Responsiveness	Linguistic Responsiveness	Cultural Responsiveness	Social-Emotional Responsiveness
Name a clear, relevant, and developmentally appropriate purpose Modify, extend, or supplement content	Use accessible, inclusive language(s) and provide definitions, examples, or visuals for new vocabulary Provide visual support for text	Reflect the cultural and social identities of students in text and visuals Incorporate student work in examples	Involve students in the creation process Incorporate the interests of students Offer support for relevant social-emotional skills and positive habits of mind

Chapter 4 Select mentor texts that. . .

Academic Responsiveness	Linguistic Responsiveness	Cultural Responsiveness	Social-Emotional Responsiveness
Are accessible to students as readers and writers Match text elements and craft moves that students can approximate	Provide support for processing, especially in multilingual texts Contain supports for language, such as labels, repetition, illustrations, definitions, or captions	Include mirrors and windows for students within the authorship, content, text, and illustrations (Sims Bishop, 1990.) Prioritize representation for those who have been historically underrepresented within the literacy world	Match relevant topics and/or interests of students with topics and story lines in the mentor texts Incorporate social-emotional support and/or positive habits of mind

Chapter 5 Provide demonstration texts that. . .

Academic Responsiveness	Linguistic Responsiveness	Cultural Responsiveness	Social-Emotional Responsiveness
Model skills that students are developing Provide multiple entry points for developing specific skills.	Mirror the structure and length of sentences students can produce Support vocabulary development through the use of definitions, visuals, and/or labels	Authentically portray the identities and experiences that are familiar and unfamiliar to students	Align with student interests and reflect shared experiences Model social-emotional skills and positive habits of mind in content or writing process

Responsiveness Across Domains available for download at **resources.corwin.com/responsivewritingteacher.**

Foreword

Everything exists in a specific context. Understanding the environment that produced a thing is critical to the understanding of that thing.

So, it is important to note that this book is emerging as we make sense of a pandemic,

While Black life is being extinguished by the state. And debated in public. And affirmed in the streets,

While there are children in cages at the border and in substandard housing across town and in crumbling schools across the tracks,

While there are "nice" people with "good" intentions whose ignorance allowed them to look the other way when policy makers voted for it to be that way,

While there are "powerful" people whose self-interest inspires them to work at keeping it that way,

While the world watches American democracy stumble over its own hubris,

While the earth itself responds to our collective failure to be good stewards of the environment with fire and superstorms and lead in the water of our most vulnerable children.

Our. Children.

We are raising them to be thoughtful, perceptive, and literate, so they see all of this. And they question us, because they are children—born truth seekers. And we have met their quest for truth with mythology disguised as education or by burying our heads in the sand altogether.

This is the real danger of our contemporary moment—that we might be raising a generation unable to grapple with the challenges that we have perpetuated ... because we are too cowardly to tell the truth, to teach the truth, and to respond to the truth.

Enlightenment thinking suggests that it is what we do in these difficult moments that will define us.

Conversely, folk wisdom sees plainly and presents a more observational truth. This historical moment has already defined us. We are a nation of bystanders.

We see injustice. We clutch pearls. We tweet. And then we sip coffee while CNN and Fox News compete for the opportunity to tell us what to do next. This is a failure of literacy. And of empathy. And, potentially, of humanity.

I am not okay with this. Neither are Melanie and Kelsey.

How we respond to what the world hands us is a lesson that resonates louder than anything that we could convey through virtual teaching or in a classroom. Our responses matter profoundly, and in this work, there is nothing more sacred than how we respond to children.

Melanie and Kelsey understand this.

They understand that being responsive to children is not platitudes or empty declarations of belief. Being responsive is work.

It is having the imagination to see beyond the status quo and the temerity to challenge it. It is the understanding that when it comes to meeting the varied needs of our children, we can work to abandon yesterday's thinking if it does not serve today's needs.

Being responsive is working to outgrow our own ideas about who children are and what they need. It is acting on the reality that reflection and introspection are impotent if they are not matched with real and sustainable ways to develop our content knowledge, grow our classroom pedagogy, and decolonize our school policy.

People often implore me to be "hopeful" for these kinds of changes.

I have studied with Melanie and Kelsey, and they remind us that hope alone is not a viable strategy for change. Hope without action is the expectation that the answers to the things that challenge us will materialize out of thin air if we simply don a positive attitude and wait. This magical thinking robs us of our agency and allows us to sidestep our responsibility to create better realities for children.

Instead, Melanie and Kelsey recontextualize hope as the catalyzing part of an active process. Hope is most powerful when it exists in relationship to careful study, collective work, thoughtful reflection, and a commitment to trying again when things do not go as planned. THIS is the recipe for the kind of human-centered transformation that we need for ourselves and for our institutions.

Melanie and Kelsey's belief in children and in their communities informs their methodology. Their outrage at injustice fuels how they confront their own thinking. Their sadness about all that we have lost has fueled purposeful teaching and deliberate engagement in a time when we need it desperately.

There are those who simply dream of a better world. And then there are those who work toward it. Melanie and Kelsey dream, AND they do the work. This book is an instructive call to action for all of us who need to be reminded of what hope enacted as classroom practice can look like.

—Cornelius Minor
Brooklyn-based dad, educator, and author of
We Got This: Equity, Access, and the Quest to Be Who Our Students Need Us to Be

Acknowledgments

We would not be a partnership without Stacey Shubitz, who merged our paths, and the entire *Two Writing Teachers* blog co-authorship team: Amy Ellerman, Betsy Hubbard, Elizabeth Moore, Kathleen Sokolowski, Lanny Ball, Marina Rodriguez, and Therapi Kaplan. Thank you for being steadfast partners in thought and in writing over the years.

Dialogue is the life-source of this book. On our first call together, Melanie told Kelsey, "Writing my first book was lonely." We are ever-grateful to our growing networks of colleagues, students, caregivers, and leaders who welcomed us as listeners and engaged in our wonderings. Because of you, this journey was never lonely. Many of you were early readers, offering critical perspectives and invaluable feedback: Tori Bachman, our proposal and draft reviewers, Rasha Hamid, Madeleine Zuck, Nazneen Patel, and Cornelius Minor. Thank you for elevating our work.

A village of educators, caregivers, and children have contributed their work and stories to this book, bringing readers in on a tour of their classrooms: Alexandra Bees und Crostin, Hayley Brown, Vicky Chau, Tien-Tien Chen, Katie Clements, Zetta Elliott, Rachel Federbush, Julia Feldman, Jennifer Frish, Rasha Hamid, Cathy Hoerle, Jordan Goff, Lisa Jacobs, Jana Julka, Linda Kim, Britt Kroll, Kara Langer, Katie Lee, Shiela Lee, Tori Leventhal, Amy Lynch, Anastasia Macris, Sally Mayas, Brekke McDowell, Shawn McGibeny, Diana Murray, Lauren Mundy, Christine Neskie, Nazneen Patel, Danielle Portnoy, Katie Rust, Shanna Schwartz, Paul Shirk, Janet Song, Rachel Strongin, Carter Swope, Jamel Toppin, Jill VanVoohis, Suzanne Vera, Dina Weiss, Allie Woodford, and Madeleine Zuck.

We had many dreams for this book, which our team at Corwin Literacy heard and honored. Tori Bachman, thank you for advocating for the colorful and consistent layout. You steered us on course, weaving together any thoughts and ideas that wandered. We are better writers, better readers, and all-around better humans because of you. Sharon Wu, we are in awe of your patience and attention to detail with delivering hundreds of images to press. Gail Buschman and the Corwin design team, and Amy Schroller—the book we hold is more beautiful, joyful, and child-centered than we ever envisioned.

From Melanie

Whenever I felt like chapters were good enough, Kelsey made them better. So much better! Kelsey combines organization and discipline with reflection and creativity, and I am privileged to write and work with her. Kelsey, thank you for making me a better writer, teacher, and thinker.

Over the years, my family has learned how to support me as a writer—delivering coffee, cookies, chocolate, or wine depending on the hour, place, or part of the process. Thanks to all of you for knowing me and loving me.

This book could not have happened without the insights and shares from the teachers and students I get to work with. As an instructional coach in many schools, there are far more than I can list here. Special shout-outs to Charlie, Julia, Naomi, Annabelle, Jack, Samantha, Natasha, and Peter—you are special writers, and I am so grateful for your contributions!

From Kelsey

Melanie, you nudged me when I needed nudging, you slowed down when I needed stillness, you offered solace in my hardest days, you wrote when I couldn't write. There were many months when you carried more weight and not for a single moment made me feel any less.

Elizabeth Schulz, I (quite literally) would not be writing this if it weren't for you. You are my compass when lost. Mom, my first teacher and editor; Dad, my first poet and best friend; you show me how to live, work, and coexist in ways that are true to one's most essential values. Joe, Heather, Jana, Kirsten, Andrew, Sam, Charlie, Ben, Jack, and Jessa: you are my home base for laughs, snuggles, and great food.

The school communities I served are imprinted in my practice and in this book. Horizon Elementary, you are at my core of responsive teaching and balanced literacy instruction. P.S. 59, you bring joy and children to the center in ways that I never knew possible. Compass Charter School, you see stakeholders as humans first, demonstrating co-construction and antiracism as a way of living. My school leaders display leadership needed in the world: Rainey Briggs, Erin Conrad, Debra Larson, Brooke Peters, Adele Schroeter, Todd Sutler, and Nekia Wise. My instructional coaches share expertise, books, and inquiries: Rasha Hamid, Jamie Mendelsohn, Gina Neumann, and Nazneen Patel. Kristi Mraz, you provided invaluable guidance toward authorship and the best doughnuts in NYC. My colleagues become family, making sure work and life are never lonely. Madeleine, I won the jackpot when you became my teaching/all-things-in-life partner.

Publisher's Acknowledgments

Corwin gratefully acknowledges the contributions of the following reviewers:

Christina Nosek
Classroom Teacher
Lucille Nixon School
Mountain View, CA

Lynn Angus Ramos
K–12 English Language Arts Coordinator
DeKalb County School District
Decatur, GA

Letter From the Authors

Dear Reader,

This book did not emerge from a place of knowing. From ideation to publication, it has been fueled by questions—questions we still do not fully have answers to:

> How can educators be responsive to students' abilities, identities, experiences, and needs?

> How can educators lean on curriculum and benchmarks while also leaning on the uniqueness of their students?

Because our process has been one of inquiry, the plans for this book have been sculpted and resculpted and then taken the shape of something completely different—something shaped by many: authors, researchers, colleagues, and children. This process, not the product we originally envisioned, nor the one you are now holding, is what we are most proud of and forever changed by.

We, like you, are constantly pushing our practice and trying to be better at inclusive practices, at reaching and engaging writers. Many curriculum guides refer to differentiation, offering alternative lessons and approaches. We needed more—a guide for aligning instruction and tools for the writers in our classrooms.

We preface what's to come by sharing the mantra that keeps us going: Don't let perfect get in the way of good. The framework, guides, tools, and stories we share are neither perfect nor complete. Perhaps there is a population we have not considered, research in the works, or another domain in which to frame responsiveness. We anticipate (and wish!) this book serves as a contribution to an ongoing dialogue that readers will expand upon and elevate.

Our intentions are this: making an abstract concept—responsiveness—more concrete. We hope the impact is this: with the strategies set forth in this book, you, too, will feel a sense of direction and preparedness in the overwhelmingly important work of responsive writing instruction.

Onward,

Melanie and Kelsey

DOMAINS OF RESPONSIVENESS

LINGUISTIC

SOCIAL-EMOTIONAL

ACADEMIC

CULTURAL

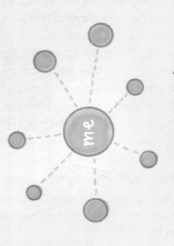

Introduction

We open this book by sharing our personal stories—how we have come to this work individually and together.

If you found Kelsey in her first years of teaching, you likely found her curriculum guides nearby—on the couch while she watched TV, on her nightstand before bed, even on her lap as she taught. Kelsey valued the teaching language and narratives suggested by curriculum writers so much that she did her best to replicate them. She told the same stories, re-created the same writing, read the same mentor texts, and crafted the same tools. Kelsey knew and delivered the curriculum *really well*. What she did not know as well, however, was herself as a writer. What she did not know as well were the writers in her classroom.

Knowing the curriculum well gave Kelsey a strong understanding of the workshop model and skills taught within each genre. It allowed her to ingrain effective teaching language for working with writers. But Kelsey's best teaching years happened when she began *referencing* curriculum instead of *memorizing* it, when she spent more time reading student writing than unit guides, when she taught with tools at her side instead of a script. The more Kelsey became present in her classroom, the more she knew the writers, and the more she knew the writers, the easier it became to be responsive in her practice. Kelsey made connections to students' lives, bringing engagement and purpose to learning. By including demonstration texts written by students in her classroom, Kelsey developed a practice of crafting her own. Kelsey found mentor texts that young writers treasured and borrowed again and again. Kids beamed, seeing their photos and writing highlighted on charts. Writing workshop buzzed with topics of excitement and passion.

When the curriculum came first, Kelsey found very little time and even less energy for the kind of work that she now realizes matters more in her quest to inspire and grow young writers:

- Reading student writing
- Establishing a professional and personal writing routine
- Planning small groups
- Studying conferring notes
- Searching for mentor texts
- Reading professional texts

When kids came first, Kelsey was able to shift the story line to the one unfolding in her curriculum guide to the one unfolding in her classroom.

Melanie's chartbooks have been a part of her teaching life for several years now. She buys blank notebooks in art supply stores—the same sort of spiral-bound notebooks that her daughters use for sketching. Melanie likes the ones with heavy covers and thick pages—slightly oversized works best for her! When she first started making charts inside of them, Melanie usually sat with the computer by her side. She'd copy resources from curriculum guides and ones shared on blogs and social media. Melanie would scroll through other people's anchor charts, strategy charts, any other visually appealing resources she could find . . . and she'd copy them into her chartbook.

DIY Literacy, by Kate Roberts and Maggie Beattie Roberts (2016), was and still is one of Melanie's favorite professional books. Since her specialty and area of responsibility is writing, Melanie tabbed the pages that had to do with writing and—you guessed it—she copied their charts. Kate and Maggie have great companion videos where they explain how to create various charts and progressions. Melanie would stop the video on a frame so that she could copy what they'd written.

Melanie's later chartbooks developed in terms of organization, as she worked to curate narrative, information, and opinion charts in separate sections. She had charts for mindsets, workshop practices, grammar and conventions, and poetry in separate sections as well. Later versions of Melanie's chartbooks even separated early primary charts from mid-elementary ones.

But the charts Melanie had acquired still weren't all *her own;* they were organized, and they were useful, but they were still copies of other people's work. And more importantly, they weren't reflective of the students in the classrooms where she worked.

It took Melanie a couple of years to realize that the pages she used over and over are the ones she created in response to a student within her own environment. Other people's beautifully illustrated charts, other people's student-specific charts, and other people's choices of mentor texts and samples of writing didn't work for Melanie. The most useful resources *for Melanie,* in reaching her writers, are the ones she's created in response to the challenges students were having right in front of her. The most useful resources for individual students are the ones she created in front of *them,* inspired by *them,* and what *they* were working on!

A Shared Story

> *My job as a teacher is to seek to understand my kids as completely as possible so that I can purposefully bend curriculum to meet them.*
>
> —Cornelius Minor (2018)

Our paths merged as coauthors of a blog: *Two Writing Teachers.* We began an ongoing dialogue that we imagine will never quite end—one in which we strive to unravel the questions that frame this book. We had many conversations before considering writing a book together—conversations about students, our communities, and our own similarities and differences. We continue to grow awareness of the intersectionality of historical and systemic racism, sexism, classism, ableism, linguicism, and so forth, as shown in Figure 0.1 (Crenshaw, 1989).

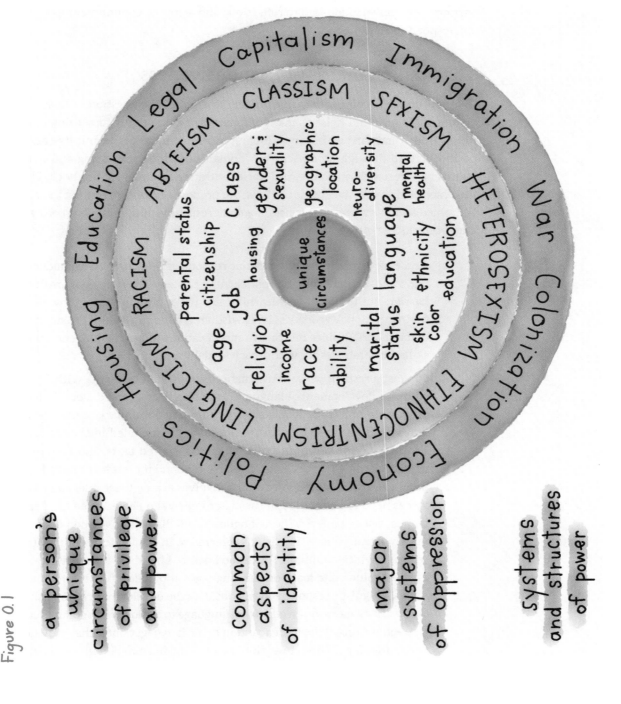

Figure 0.1

a person's unique circumstances of privilege and power

common aspects of identity

major systems of oppression

systems and structures of power

We recognize our privileges as white educators, reflecting upon and acknowledging moments in which such privileges have caused harm—in the classroom, in schools, and beyond. Together, our teaching experience ranges from schools in predominantly white, middle- to upper-class suburban communities to socioeconomically and racially diverse urban communities. *This work has mattered in each of these settings in many different ways.* We share successes and failures, new learning and struggles, inroads and barriers. Our conversations led to reflections and a greater commitment to knowing and responding to writers.

The Four Domains of Responsiveness

"But *how* do we become responsive writing teachers?" The question hung in the air on one of Melanie and Kelsey's many phone calls. Adamant for something tangible, Kelsey (the visual partner) began scribbling boxes and notes as Melanie (the auditory partner) talked through processes. Four domains emerged, anchoring and weaving together the research, structure, and stories within the chapters of this book. Though the practice of responsiveness is not new, we propose responsive writing instruction be framed as *academic responsiveness*, *linguistic responsiveness*, *cultural responsiveness*, and *social-emotional responsiveness*.

1. *Academic responsiveness:* Academic responsiveness begins with understanding where students are in their learning process—the skills that are firm, the barriers in the way of new learning, and the entry points that provide access for instruction. Vygotsky's (1978) wisdom around the zone of proximal development (ZPD) guides responsive modifications to instruction, ensuring that skills and strategies are within each student's reach.

2. *Linguistic responsiveness:* Linguistic responsiveness begins with knowing students' development of language, home language(s) and dialect(s), language processing, and content-related structures and vocabulary so that the many ways children communicate are honored and included in the community. The languages used in instruction, charts, shared texts, and mentor texts matter, vitally, to the accessibility of content and representation students experience. Linguistic responsiveness involves asking these questions: Whose voices need to be uplifted in the classroom? Who needs to see their spoken language(s) on paper? Whose languages and dialects have been historically marginalized? When "English" is referred to in academic discourse, it often refers to white-dominant *Academic English*. Linguistic responsiveness recognizes, values, and leans on the languages and dialects of children in classrooms. Linguistic responsiveness considers the development of English as an *expansion* of aperture, an *additional* language to deploy when communicating through writing. It does not abandon home languages but rather provides opportunities for children to explore nuance and imagination in home languages and then provides support for processes of code-switching, translating, and expressing with the same effectiveness and voice in English.

3. *Cultural responsiveness:* Cultural responsiveness begins with recognizing, honoring, and reflecting diverse cultural and social identities and experiences. In school communities that are racially diverse, this builds a sense of

authentic belonging for students within authorship and within the content of books. In school communities that are predominantly white, this widens and recenters the scope in which literacy is conveyed in the world, combating racialized and stereotypical narratives. Across school communities, representation and inclusion matter while working to build equitable environments and empathetic citizens (Gloria Ladson-Billings, Sonia Nieto, Zaretta Hammond).

4. *Social-emotional responsiveness:* Social-emotional responsiveness begins with honoring the whole child: interests, the social-emotional tendencies, and habits of mind. Each of these areas is then integrated in the writing process and thus contribute to students' identities as writers.

Type of Responsiveness		Description
Academic responsiveness		*Ensuring new skills and content match students' abilities and goals*
Linguistic responsiveness		*Ensuring language(s) used in instruction and in the classroom environment are accessible and inclusive of home languages*
Cultural responsiveness		*Ensuring a diverse representation of authorship and within the content of texts*
Social-emotional responsiveness		*Ensuring a safe and supportive environment for taking risks and overcoming challenges in the writing process*

We will refer to and expand upon the following chart throughout the following chapters and sections.

The Structure of This Book

While composing the academic, linguistic, cultural, and social-emotional canvas of a classroom, teachers collect data, modify or create plans, construct tools, and provide texts for support—all while being responsible for a classroom full of children and a day filled with other content areas. We recognize the organizational, emotional, and logistical challenge of this through firsthand experience.

"What do I need?" you might ask. "Where do I begin?" In each chapter, you'll find starting points, places to return to, and a consistent structure. You might take some of the tools and use them just the way we've created them. You might also find inspiration in the thought processes and stories of teachers that we have shared. We urge you not to try to do everything at once. Rather, begin with aspects of instruction and responsiveness that are most needed and most relevant for students in *your classroom* so that you modify and create tools for your own assessments, plans, and instruction.

The sequence of chapters aligns with components of writing instruction: *assessment, planning, charts, mentor texts,* and *demonstration texts.* Within each of these chapters, there are actionable steps, tools, classroom examples, resources, and tips for responsiveness across the four domains, ones that we hope communicate clarity, purpose, and joy. Each chapter ends with an example to portray the integration of the domains in practice. You will find a downloadable, printable template for every chart online at resources.corwin.com/responsivewritingteacher.

Chapter 6 outlines a shift in each of these instructional components from teacher-driven to student-driven (peer-driven and self-driven), which is, we suggest, the highest level of responsiveness—one that fosters agency and empowerment. While this book was started before March of 2020, we were revising it throughout the COVID-19 pandemic and the widespread movement against systemic oppression and structural racism sparked by the murders of Breonna Taylor and George Floyd. These events pushed us forward in our thinking about how to engage students in work that is meaningful, actionable, and healing—and how we might do this even without sharing a physical space.

We build upon each element of writing instruction from a foundation of our own beliefs about best practices. We hold steadfast to the structure writing workshop, leaning on the work of Donald Graves (1983)—students need instruction as well as time for independent practice and choice in topic. We hold steadfast to the importance of a literacy-rich environment, as described by Lucy Calkins (1986/2008)—an environment in which tools and resources support student learning. We hold steadfast to a framework of balanced literacy, an important component being the balance of small- and whole-group instruction as well as direct instruction and the curriculum of talk (Fisher, Frey, & Akhavan, 2019)—in which each day is structured to include interactive writing, shared writing, small-group instruction, and independent writing. We hold steadfast to the interconnectedness of reading and writing; students learn to write from studying the craft moves of published authors (Dorfman & Capelli, 2017). Finally, and possibly most important, we hold steadfast to the simultaneous engagement of teachers as writers—to the deep understanding, authenticity, and empathy that is cultivated when teachers are writers.

It is our hope that this book will provide you with the tools you need to be a responsive writing teacher for the young writers in your classroom and that you will make these tools your own as you become more comfortable with these concepts and with the children in your care.

The Importance of Word Choice and Nuances

Words carry implicit messages and are especially important when working in communities and with children. Though we continue to unpack language used in the education realm, here a few relevant revisions made while writing:

- *Multilingual:* In an episode of the *Leading Equity* podcast titled "A Discussion on Linguistic Equity With Dr. Barbara (BK) Kennedy," host Dr. Sheldon Eakins (2020) expressed that referring to students as English learners or English language learners "privileges those who are English speakers first. Obviously, that's a deficit mindset that we're perpetuating." Therefore, within the linguistic domain, we have maintained the lens and terminology of students who are multilingual and on a continuum of Academic English proficiency.

- *Home language(s):* In efforts to expand and recenter language considerations from white-dominant Academic English, we use *home language(s)* when referring to language(s) children speak outside of school.

- *Inclusive language:* In this book, on tools, in stories, while teaching language, and in communication with families, we consider the inclusiveness of language, including *home* instead of *house*, *grown-ups* or *caregivers* instead of *parents*, *writers* instead of *boys and girls,* and gender-neutral pronouns (e.g., *they/them*).

- *"My students" and other possessive language use:* Kelsey had a conversation with LaToya Nelson (personal communication, April 2020), a friend and expert on trauma-informed practices, who nudged our thinking around languages and actions that implies ownership of children. We revised *our* students with *students in* our *classrooms.*

- *Use of* we: During the Coaching for Equity conference in February 2020 (hosted by the NYC Leadership Academy), Derrick Spaulding challenged attendees to monitor their use of *we* as opposed to *I.* The use of the plural first person can imply an assumption. In this book and in other areas of our lives, we—Kelsey and Melanie—have tried to increase our awareness of when we use first-person plural, making sure that we are using it with intention and agreement.

- *Language that centers dominant groups:* We've revised *children in front of us* to *children alongside us* after Kelsey asked, "Who does that phrase center?" We are also cognizant of the use of any language that intends *other* for the same reason, such as the term *diverse,* which centers whiteness, as explained by Chad Everett (2017) in "There Is No Diverse Book," on his blog, *ImagineLit.*

- *Capitalizing Black:* Alexandria Neason, from the *Columbia Journalism Review*, explains, "I view the term *Black* as both a recognition of an ethnic identity in the States that doesn't rely on hyphenated Americanness . . . and is also transnational and inclusive of our Caribbean [and] Central/South American siblings . . . . *African American* is not wrong, and some prefer it, but if we are going to capitalize *Asian* and *South Asian* and *Indigenous,* for example, groups that include myriad ethnic identities united by shared race and geography and, to some degree, culture, then we also have to capitalize *Black"* (Laws, 2020).

- *Person-first and asset-based language:* After attending a session at the 2018 NCTE Annual Convention with M. Colleen Cruz, we are cognizant of language that implies a deficit. Continuously, we avoid the attachment labels or identities on children and therefore use *children/students who are/who have* whenever possible.

CHAPTER 1

Collecting Information About the Writers in Your Classroom

Knowing the writers of a classroom community is one of the most important elements of instruction. Knowing writers—within and beyond the classroom—allows for responsive instruction, engaging resources, and inclusive texts. In a classroom where they are known, seen, and honored, children can feel safe taking risks, making mistakes, and learning from places of support and inspiration.

When the school year ended, Kelsey brought home a collection of classroom plants to care for over the summer. Her instinct was to immediately begin tending to the plants—pruning, watering, repotting. She was eager to place them around her Brooklyn apartment. But before she could do that, she needed more information. In her first year of indoor gardening, Kelsey lost a lot of plants: plants that rotted due to overwatering, plants that developed fungi due to humidity, plants that did not get enough air circulation because they were placed too high, and plants that burned from intense sunlight. In each of those situations, Kelsey's plants did not grow as she had hoped—not due to a lack of care but due to *unideal* care. With a local plant expert's words in mind—"Mimic the environment it naturally thrives in"—Kelsey knew she needed to know more about each unique plant and its history before tending to it.

Why Collecting Information Matters

The National Equity Project (NEP; n.d.) defines three aspects of equity in schools:

- Ensuring equally high outcomes for all participants in our educational system; removing the predictability of success or failures that currently correlates with any social or cultural factor;
- Interrupting inequitable practices, examining biases, and creating inclusive multicultural school environments for adults and children; and
- Discovering and cultivating the unique gifts, talents, and interests that every human possesses.

These three points drive the work of this book: striving for high outcomes for all students while also creating inclusive environments that respond to and center them. Just as Kelsey learned to cultivate the unique needs of her plants, the domains of responsiveness lead us to the unique gifts, talents, and interests of the writers in classrooms.

When students join classrooms, teachers typically know *some* information about them: names, languages, date of birth, addresses, and academic records from the previous year. Upon meeting students, educators can begin filling in the gaps of what is known, and often, this data collection is in the context of skills—what writers can *do*. Formal and informal assessment measures show students' writing skills and allow for decisions to be made about instruction in order to lift those skills to the next level.

These surface-level assessments are, of course, valuable. Observing writers and their work provides information that helps form instructional plans. However, other essential information is not visible on such assessments: cultural practices, family structures, mindsets, emotional tendencies, defining experiences, identities (as writers and as humans), home language(s) and language development, interests, and friends. There is *so much more* to learn about students than the skills that transfer to paper, and in order to learn about students, we must become *habitual* and *intentional information collectors*: asking questions, seeking stories, observing mindfully, and listening intently.

Teachers can use assessment practices to make decisions about the effectiveness and adjustments needed for instruction (Supovitz, 2012) as well as gathering information about students' thought processes. When teachers study students' progress, or lack thereof, they can adjust and refine, leading to better learning.

In this chapter, we explore information that goes beyond numbers and letters and labels. Such information informs and anchors each decision that follows, allowing one to curate an ideal environment in which children thrive.

Ways to Collect Information

Formative and Summative Data Collection

Collecting information about students serves two major purposes:

1. To inform practice (formative data collection)
2. To measure learning growth (summative data collection)

The tools we suggest for collecting data in this chapter help to answer these questions:

- What do students need to know?
- What will engage them in learning?
- What entry points will make the work accessible and relevant so that students can apply skills independently in and beyond our classrooms?

There are a number of ways to gather information about students. Throughout this chapter, we will share a variety of methods that encompass summative and formative data collection.

Summative methods are used to collect information about students' progress toward acquiring specific skills and behaviors, typically following instruction. This kind of information informs how effective instruction was for the class and individual students.

Formative methods, in turn, are used to plan instruction based on students' progress toward specific goals. A formative assessment "is a planned, ongoing process used by all students and teachers during learning and teaching to elicit and use evidence of student learning to improve student understanding of intended disciplinary outcomes and support students to become self-directed learners" (Formative Assessment for Students and Teachers [FAST] State Collaborative on Assessment and Student Standards [SCASS], 2011). As such, this kind of data collection happens throughout a writing unit, allowing for responsive decisions for instruction.

Trumbull and Lash (2013) explain formative assessment as any instructional activity that uncovers how students think about what is being taught and improves their learning. In a May 2018 interview with Jim Knight, Zaretta Hammond adds that formative assessment "helps students become conscious of their learning moves and how to change them to improve their learning" (Knight, 2018).

With purpose and intentionality in data collection, there grows a shift from focusing solely on what students know and can do to what methods of instruction fuel the greatest progress for them. This information, in particular, is what drives next steps.

Formative Data Collection	Summative Data Collection
Helps to answer this question: *How can students learn more effectively?*	Helps to answer this question: *Was instruction effective?*
Is typically unscored	Is typically scored, using a points system, rubric, or progression
Takes place *during* instruction, often more than once during a unit	Takes place *after* instruction
Is used by both teachers *and* students to make adjustments in the learning process	Is used mostly by teachers and/or administrators to assess overall learning that happened

Formative and summative assessments can become a routine component of instruction. In Chapter 2, we recommend including assessments as a component of weekly and unit plans. Many of the methods for data collection in the following table can be integrated in daily, weekly, or unit plans.

Formative Data Collection in Writing	Summative Data Collection in Writing
Preassessments	On-demand writing pieces
Observations	Student work in writing folders
Questionnaires	Presentations such speeches, oral reports, or readings
Checklists	Performance tasks
Discussions	
Conferences	
Turn and talks	
Notebook entries	
Reflections	
Exit slips	

The Importance of Observations

Observational methods for collecting data, otherwise known as *kidwatching*, is an important type of formative assessment and can happen throughout the school day, informally, and formally—with an intentional observational lens planned for specific groups of children.

Speaking with and observing a child leads to some of the most valuable information, and this is certainly not limited to times of the day devoted to writing. Making it a ritual to record these moments allows teachers to hold on to them for future planning, considering these questions:

- What do students do as part of their learning process?
- How do they develop ideas?
- What do they do with those ideas?
- What engages them? What disengages them?

Yetta Goodman (1985), a professor and researcher at the University of Arizona, writes extensively about kidwatching and has established frameworks for engaging in systematic observations of children as they learn literacy skills. What do students know? How do they use that knowledge? What do they do when they are frustrated or unsure of themselves? These types of questions can become part of the repertoire as we watch and learn about children.

Some educators prefer to keep records of observational notes in an open-ended journal, while other educators prefer to use templates or organized notebooks, with organized sections for each student.

Tip for Tomorrow

The process of data collection and analysis can be overwhelming. We've found that the more time-consuming assessments are, the less time is available for thoughtful planning around data. We recommend that any scheduled windows for data collection be followed by scheduled time to plan how to use that data and plan responsive instruction—it's even better if this can be done alongside colleagues!

Data Collection Across the Four Domains

Throughout this chapter, we share systems and structures that have been helpful to K–5 teachers. We emphasize collecting information about students across each domain: *academic* responsiveness, *linguistic* responsiveness, *cultural* responsiveness, and *social-emotional* responsiveness. As with each chapter that follows, there are options and entry points for the work that is presented.

The information that is gathered here is referenced throughout the rest of this book (and may be at your side as you plan and teach!). It's critical to remember that data is not only gathered to inform; it is gathered to inform instruction.

We are not suggesting that you utilize everything at once!

You might make it a goal to use or re-create one tool from each domain. Alternatively, you might collect information from different domains at different parts of a unit or the school year, with the specific needs of your students in mind. It's important that whatever you use to gather information works for you, your students, your curriculum, and related goals for each.

Academic Responsiveness ↓	Linguistic Responsiveness ↓	Cultural Responsiveness ↓	Social-Emotional Responsiveness ↓
Collect information about . . .			
Students' proficiency with content-related skills Writing-related behaviors as students engage in a writing process	Students' home language(s), speaking and processing skills, language use, and vocabulary development	The cultural and social identities of students	Student interests within and outside of school The social-emotional tendencies of students in relation to writing

COLLECTING INFORMATION FOR ACADEMIC RESPONSIVENESS

Melanie was working in a classroom, supporting the teacher with getting ready to launch a narrative writing unit. They wanted to get to know students as writers more before making plans. They were curious about information they could collect as students selected paper, so they decided to observe students at the writing center, where several paper choices were available. Melanie and the teacher quickly sketched a grid to take notes and then framed their observations with questions:

- Will they choose paper with several lines?
- How many pieces of paper will they take at once?
- Do they know how to use a stapler and set up story booklets for themselves?

Academic Responsiveness ↓
Collect information about . . .
Students' proficiency with content-related skills
Writing-related behaviors as students engage in a writing process

It was fascinating to watch what and how students chose:

- One writer got a set of papers for the next great American novel but had a hard time getting started.
- Another writer took a single sheet of paper with the biggest picture box available, which allowed space to show detailed illustrations and labels.
- Many writers excitedly reached for new prestapled booklets with more lines than had been offered before, showing an increase in volume.
- A few writers added multiple blank books to their folders. Other writers returned to the writing center to staple additional pages or books they needed.

The information gathered during this observation not only offered valuable insight about each writer and their process but also led to more responsive plans for the narrative unit and differentiated support.

Collecting Information About Content-Related Skills

By practice, the most abundant kind of data teachers collect is related to academic growth. Many schools require this kind of data, sharing it with families and using it to measure student growth alongside standardized benchmarks. Data collected for this domain can be referenced when planning for whole-group and small-group instruction.

In any given writing unit, it's important to know the skills and concepts students acquire following instruction. It can be helpful to keep those written or charted in one place. That way, it's easier to check and cross-check learning that is happening at any point in the unit. This information is vital to have on hand during conferring sessions with students. You can quickly glance at skill(s) that a student is working on, and target those skills in your conference.

Many state assessments and curriculum guides score writing within the following components:

→ Structure: Is the student able to establish a beginning, middle, and end?
→ Development: Is the student able to use various strategies of elaboration to develop the text?
→ Conventions: What grade-level conventions are students using to compose and edit their writing?

One way to collect information within the academic domain is to define grade-level goals within (or beyond) these components, then determine indicators that writers are exceeding, meeting, or approaching each goal.

Chart 1.1 can be used to collect information about student proficiency with writing skills. The first template is for recording qualities of structure, development, and language conventions that are exceeding, meeting, or approaching grade-level standards. The second template is for recording information about students who are exceeding, meeting, or approaching grade-level standards.

Use this tool if . . . you need to know whether students are exceeding, meeting, or approaching expectations for specific skills. This is helpful to do or reference in preparation for caregiver-teacher conferences, data meetings, or a new genre study.

Revisit this tool . . . several times across a unit—as a preassessment before a unit begins (using an on-demand sample of writing), as a mid-unit assessment (several weeks later), and as a postassessment (after a unit ends). It can be helpful for monitoring growth to use the same copy of the tool to record information across a unit, so we've included space for three different assessment dates; make it your own by adding as many dates as you need.

To use this tool, you will need . . . to determine what qualities of structure, development, and language conventions are exceeding, meeting, or approaching grade-level expectations. You will also need to collect student writing samples or look across writing in writing folders. It's ideal if this becomes a weekly practice, but aiming for every other week will allow you to collect information at the beginning, middle, and end of a unit that is about six weeks long.

Make this tool your own by . . . narrowing in on one or two goals for structure, development, and language conventions that most closely match the goals of your students and are aligned with any curricular or school-wide goals. We recommend using the Common Core State Standards (CCSS) in addition to curriculum guides when determining grade-level expectations with colleagues.

CHART 1.1

COLLECTING INFORMATION ABOUT WRITING SKILLS

Genre of Writing/Unit of Study: Opinion Writing, Grade 2

STRUCTURE	DEVELOPMENT	LANGUAGE CONVENTIONS
Grade-Level Expectations:	**Grade-Level Expectations:**	**Grade-Level Expectations:**
Exceeding	**Exceeding**	**Exceeding**
Hook readers into caring about the opinion in the beginning and ending.	Name more than two reasons with several sentences supporting each.	Spell more high-frequency words correctly than are presently on the word wall and/or edit to fix words spelled incorrectly.
Meeting	**Meeting**	**Meeting**
Convince readers of the opinion in the beginning and ending.	Name two reasons with several sentences supporting each.	Spell word wall words correctly.
Approaching	**Approaching**	**Approaching**
State the opinion in beginning and ending.	Name one or two reasons without supporting sentences.	Spell some word wall words correctly.

(Continued)

(Continued)

FUNCTIONING AREA *Jot notes as you need them for all three.*	STRUCTURE **Grade-Level Expectations:** Convince readers of the opinion in the beginning and ending.	DEVELOPMENT **Grade-Level Expectations:** Name at least two reasons with several sentences supporting each.	LANGUAGE CONVENTIONS **Grade-Level Expectations:** Spell word wall words correctly.
DATE: First piece written before instruction begins (first week of May)			
Exceeding	Kierra Charlie Alex	Kierra Alex Thomas Michael	
Meeting	Thomas Michael Seth Mara Kate Sanara Amar Dean Kyron Olivia Sophia TJ Sanique	Charlie Seth Olivia Sophia Sanique Rashad	Charlie Alex Mara Kate Sanara Kendra Sanique Kathleen Kierra Michael Olivia Sophia
Approaching	Rashad Kathleen Manu Alex Kate Kendra	Mara Kate Sanara Amar Dean Kyron TJ Kathleen Manu Michael Kendra (Note for area of focus: extend sequence of lessons for development)	Amar Dean Samar TJ Rashad Manu

DATE: Third week of May (look at student writing folders)			
Exceeding			
Meeting			
Approaching			

DATE: First week of June (look at published piece)			
Exceeding			
Meeting			
Approaching			

Caption: A teacher prepared this chart to prepare for an opinion writing unit. After the preassessment, they filled in students' names and will continue to update it as the unit continues.

online resources ↘ Available for download at **resources.corwin.com/responsivewritingteacher.**

Collecting Information About Writing Behaviors and Writing Processes

Knowing *how* writers write is as valuable as knowing *what* they can write. Thinking back to Goodman's work, kidwatching is imperative for collecting this kind of information. In this section, we provide tools for collecting information about writing processes and writing behaviors.

Writing Processes	Writing Behaviors
How students move through the writing process (nonsequential, nonlinear)	*What students do as they move through the writing process*
• Generating ideas • Organizing and planning • Drafting • Revising • Editing • Publishing	• Writing task initiation • Volume • Stamina • Focus • Use of classroom tools • Engagement during instruction • Response to feedback • Sharing of work

The writing process is often illustrated as a cycle, like Figure 1.1:

Figure 1.1

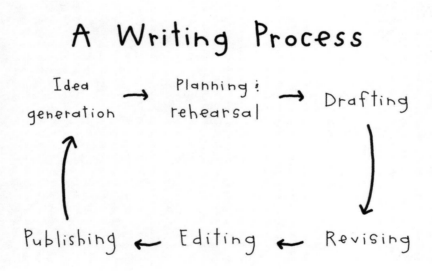

However, this cycle varies for each writer. Donald Graves (1985/2020), who was a professor of education and researcher of how children learn to write, emphasized the individuality of various processes: "When children use a meaning-centered approach to writing, they compose in idiosyncratic ways. Each child's approach to composing is different from the next." Writers flow through the process in different ways and spend varying amounts of time in each phase. When writing this book together, Melanie and Kelsey were constantly reminded of this.

Kelsey's writing process looks something like Figure 1.2, whereas Melanie's process looks something like Figure 1.3. You may notice that Kelsey spends much more time in the idea generation and planning phase as she writes. Melanie drafts as she plans, and her process leads to more ideas. She spends a lot of time editing and revising as she continues to draft. Neither Kelsey nor Melanie complete the entire draft before revising and editing.

Figure 1.2

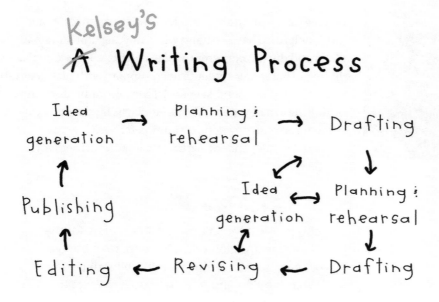

Figure 1.3

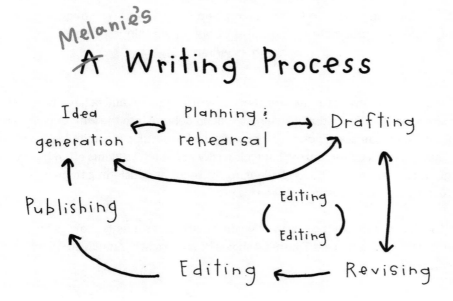

With this in mind, it's important to name and teach into each part of the writing process—offering strategies and supports along the way. When sketching or teaching about the process of writing, flexibility can be shown by saying, "For some writers, the writing process looks like this . . . for some writers, the writing process looks like this. It's important that writers do each of these things, but writers can do them in many different ways." In Chapter 6, we share ways for students to grow ownership of understanding their writing process.

Having information about students' writing processes and behaviors is helpful to have on hand when making unit and small-group plans and during conferences with writers. For example, if you discover that many students need support with idea generation, you can plan to spend several lessons on brainstorming at the beginning of a new genre study. Similarly, if you know that many students are still developing stamina for writing, you could plan to break up independent writing time with partner work.

Tip for Tomorrow

Try not to engage in any interactions or conferences for the first few minutes after instruction ends. Instead, take the time to observe how students get to work during their independent writing time. What they do and how they do it is valuable information for next instructional steps and high-level learning.

You can say, "Writers, as you get started on your own writing, I am going to learn from you. I am going to watch to see all of the things you do to think, plan, and start writing. You might even notice me taking notes about all the things you are doing as writers."

When addressing any of the areas within the writing process and behaviors, whether in a small group or individually, we recommend delving into the *why* as well as the solution. You might say, "I notice that you stop writing after a few minutes. Is writing for a long time tricky for you? What feels tricky about it?" Students often have great insight into what makes things challenging for them, and including them in the process of strategy-making is an empowering process.

Chart 1.2 helps with looking closely at writing behaviors students show as they move through the writing process. Figure 1.4 shows how one teacher modified this chart for specific needs.

Use this tool if . . . you are wondering which writing behaviors are areas of strength and challenge for students.

Revisit this tool . . . regularly throughout the unit. Kidwatching is a powerful practice that can inform instruction.

To use this tool, you will need . . . to observe writers during independent writing time and look across student work in writing folders.

Make this tool your own by . . . knowing that the behaviors can be interchanged or expanded upon the components selected depending on what is most relevant to your own writers. You might collect information about student independence and/or proficiency compared to grade-level goals related to the following:

- Initiating writing tasks
- Showing volume
- Demonstrating stamina
- Maintaining focus in work
- Using classroom tools
- Being engaged during instruction

CHART 1.2
COLLECTING INFORMATION ABOUT WRITING BEHAVIORS

Focus of Study: _____

	WRITING BEHAVIOR: Collecting Materials	**WRITING BEHAVIOR:** Getting Started	**WRITING BEHAVIOR:** Staying on Task
Needs little to no support or reminders	Kierra Charlie Alex Thomas Michael Seth Mara Kate Sanara Amar	Kierra Charlie Alex Thomas Michael Seth Mara TJ	Kierra Charlie Alex Dean Rashad

(Continued)

(Continued)

	WRITING BEHAVIOR: Collecting Materials	WRITING BEHAVIOR: Getting Started	WRITING BEHAVIOR: Staying on Task
Needs some support and/or occasional reminders	Dean Kyron Olivia Sophia Sanique Manu Alex Kate Kendra	Kate Sanara Amar Kyron Olivia Kate Kendra	Kate Sanara Amar Kyron Olivia Kathleen Sophia Sanique
Needs continuous support and/or many reminders	TJ Rashad Kathleen	Rashad Kathleen Sophia Sanique Manu Alex	TJ Manu Alex Kate Kendra

online resources 🔍 Available for download at **resources.corwin.com/responsivewritingteacher.**

Figure 14 Example of Collecting Information About Writing Behaviors

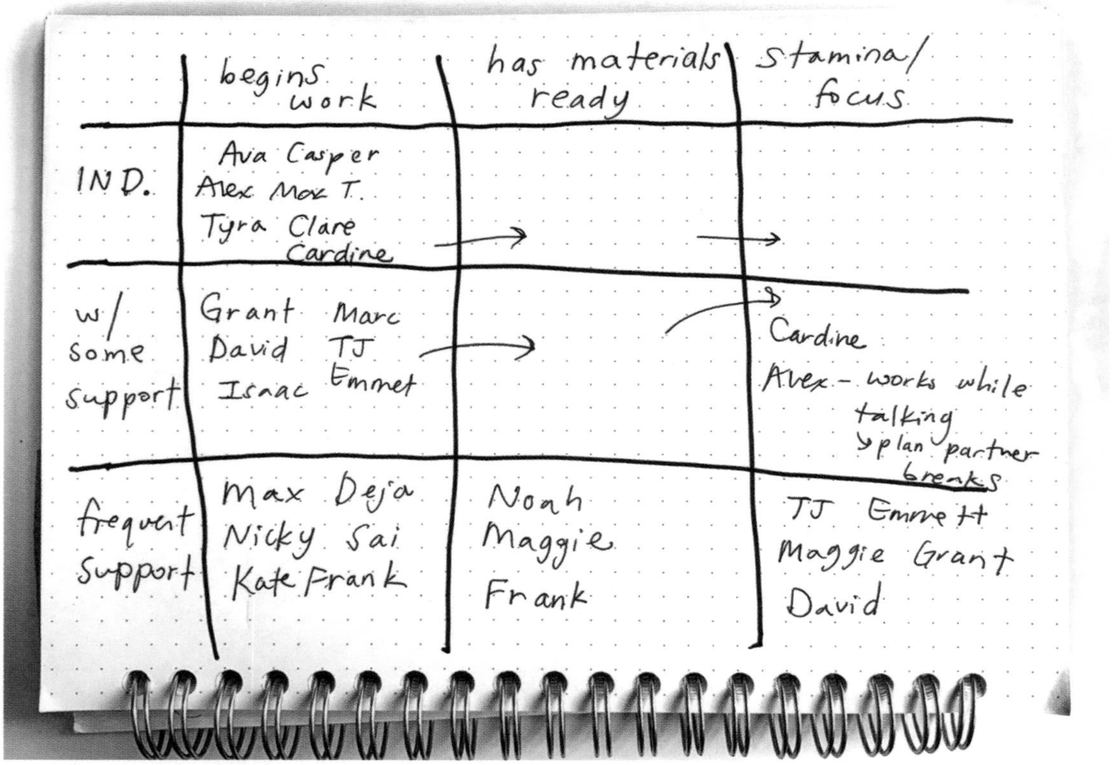

This chart was filled out in the first five minutes following instruction in an upper-grade classroom, as students transitioned into independent writing time. This now serves as formative data to support important small-group instruction around getting to work, having materials ready to go, and staying focused as writers.

Chart 1.3 helps with learning about students' individual writing processes. Figure 1.5 shows an example of a modified version of this chart.

Use this tool if . . . you are wondering which aspects of the writing process students have as strengths and areas of challenge.

Revisit this tool . . . every four to six weeks or once during each unit.

To use this tool, you will need . . . to observe writers during independent writing time and look across student work in writing folders.

Make this tool your own by . . . narrowing the focus to a specific aspect (or several specific aspects) of the writing process. For example, at the beginning of a unit, or before a new unit, you can observe students during the beginning of independent writing and record information about how they generate ideas. You can also use this tool to track which phase of the writing process students spend the most amount of time in or frequently return to.

Figure 1.5 Example of a Second-Grade Teacher's Collecting Information About Students' Writing Processes Chart

A teacher listed student names and notes to prepare for small-group instruction and individual support.

CHART 1.3

COLLECTING INFORMATION ABOUT STUDENTS' WRITING PROCESSES

Focus of Study: Information

Date: January 2019

	IDEA GENERATING	ORGANIZING AND PLANNING	WRITING/ DRAFTING	EDITING	REVISING
Strength for:	Kierra	Kierra	Kierra	Kierra	Alex
	Charlie	Charlie	Charlie	Charlie	Sanique
	Alex	Alex	Alex	Sanique	Olivia
	Thomas	Thomas	Olivia	Thomas	Sanara
	Michael	Michael	Sanara	Michael	Amar
	Mara	Seth	Amar	Mara	Dean
	Kate	Sanara	Dean	Kate	Kendra
	Sanara	Amar	TJ	Sanara	Olivia
	Amar	Dean	Rashad		
	Dean	TJ	Kathleen		
	Kyron	Rashad	Manu		
	TJ	Kathleen	Kendra		
	Rashad	Manu	Sophia		
	Kathleen	Kendra	Sanique		
	Kendra		Kyron		
	Olivia		Mara		
	Sanique				
Challenge for:	Amar	Olivia	Thomas	Amar	TJ
	Seth	Sophia	Michael	Dean	Rashad
	Sophia	Sanique	Seth	Alex	Kierra
	Manu	Kyron	Kate	Kyron	Charlie
		Mara		TJ	Kathleen
		Kate		Rashad	Seth
				Kathleen	Sophia
				Manu	Manu
				Olivia	Amar

online resources 🔖 Available for download at **resources.corwin.com/responsivewritingteacher.**

COLLECTING INFORMATION FOR LINGUISTIC RESPONSIVENESS

Hana moved to her new school from Korea in March, knowing only a few words in English. The English as an additional language (EAL) specialist worked with Hana on a formal state language assessment, then enlisted the support of a translator to learn about Hana's native language development. She discovered that Hana could already read and write in Korean. Hana's teacher gathered additional information by corresponding, via email, with Hana's mom. The first priority was making sure that Hana was able to communicate physiological needs.

Linguistic Responsiveness ↓
Collect information about . . .
Students' home language(s), speaking and processing skills, language use, and vocabulary development

The next priority was driven by Hana, who returned home from school each day and asked to learn words in English that she wanted to say to her new friends: *Hula-Hoop, slide, color, play with me, chase.* Hana's classmates went home with similar research questions: *How do you count to ten in Korean? How do you say "I love you"?*

The teacher observed the motivation of both Hana and the other students to communicate as friends (they creatively found ways to do this with American Sign Language, gestures, and visuals), which became the most valuable information gathered. The classroom teacher, EAL specialist, and Hana's mom (and Hana!) worked collaboratively for the remainder of the school year: sharing notes and ideas from various language assessments, observations, and conversations. This supported Hana's English language acquisition and the class's Korean language acquisition, and empowered students to strengthen social bonds.

Collecting Information About Students' Home Language(s) Speaking and Processing Skills, Language Use, and Vocabulary Development

Language is one of the most powerful tools a writer has to tell stories, to persuade, to teach, or to inspire. Additionally, regardless of content area, language invites learners to access instruction. Within the context of writing, there are three ways in which we consider linguistic abilities:

- For students who speak additional language(s) at home
- For students who receive speech-and language-related services
- For all students as they build vocabulary and content-specific language structures, as well as develop grammar skills

During the 2019 NCTE Annual Convention, April Baker-Bell copresented a session that Melanie attended, titled "Dismantling White Supremacy in Critical Teacher Inquiry: Humanizing Black and Brown Youths in English Education."

"What is the language education that we offer Black students?" she asked, pointing out that "most Black and brown children have a disadvantage because their language is not the academic language."

Baker-Bell's (2020) recently published book, *Linguistic Justice,* provides an antiracist Black Language pedagogy, which English language arts teachers can implement in efforts to dismantle anti-Black linguistic racism. In this approach, which centers Black linguistic liberation, Baker-Bell "introduces a new way forward . . . that intentionally and unapologetically centers the linguistic, cultural, racial, intellectual, and self-confidence needs of Black students."

If a students' home language is dismissed or corrected as "improper," it erases that aspect of their linguistic and cultural identity. It's not enough to bring Black children to the table of white dominance in literacy instruction (and beyond). We must also draw educators and children from dominant groups to tables in which they are not the center.

Following any aspect of information collection entails a necessary immersion for educators—engaging in similar writing processes (academic), exploring neighborhoods and cultures (cultural), and familiarizing oneself with topics of interest (social-emotional). Linguistic responsiveness means learning the norms of languages students speak at home. Without doing so, it can be difficult to be successful in instruction—in *hearing* students, in communicating with them, and in supporting code-switching and translation processes.

Experts of language development in schools, such as speech and language providers and English as additional language specialists, are essential collaborators for collecting information and planning. The assessments that are given by service providers are done with far greater comprehensiveness and lead to more targeted goals.

When working with students who are multilingual, it helps to know and understand the stages of English language acquisition (Hill & Björk, 2008; Krashen & Terrell, 1983, 2000; Mahnke, 1985). It's also important to remember that the process of language development varies for each individual, depending on a number of factors, including strength of students' first language (Robertson & Ford, 2008).

Chart 1.4 can help identify where students are in the process of acquiring English.

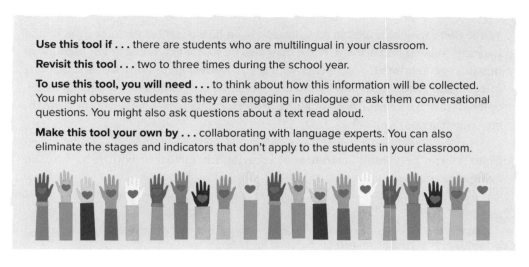

Use this tool if . . . there are students who are multilingual in your classroom.

Revisit this tool . . . two to three times during the school year.

To use this tool, you will need . . . to think about how this information will be collected. You might observe students as they are engaging in dialogue or ask them conversational questions. You might also ask questions about a text read aloud.

Make this tool your own by . . . collaborating with language experts. You can also eliminate the stages and indicators that don't apply to the students in your classroom.

CHART 1.4

DETERMINING STAGES OF THE DEVELOPMENT OF ENGLISH AS AN ADDITIONAL LANGUAGE

STUDENTS	STAGE	INDICATORS
	Preproduction	• Minimal comprehension • Little or no verbalization • Nods yes and no • Draws and points
Rashan	Early production	• Limited comprehension • One- or two-word responses • Uses key words and familiar phrases • Uses present tense verbs
	Speech emergence	• Good comprehension • Simple sentences • Grammar and pronunciation errors • Misunderstandings of jokes and figurative language
Amar TJ	Beginning fluency	• Fluent in social situations • Gaps in vocabulary • Gaps in appropriate phrases, especially as they relate to academic speech
Seth Manu	Intermediate fluency	• Excellent comprehension • Few grammatical errors
Kierra Sanara	Advanced fluency	• Near-native level of speech

online resources 🔖 Available for download at **resources.corwin.com/responsivewritingteacher.**

Receptive and expressive language development also plays a role in students' writing. People use receptive language to understand what is said. People use expressive language to share thoughts, ideas, and feelings (American Speech-Language-Hearing Association, n.d.). When students are developing receptive language skills, it can impact the effectiveness of instruction. When students are still developing expressive language skills, it can impact the effectiveness of writing.

While there may be students who already have IEPs classified under a speech- and language-related impairment, there may also be students who have not yet had an impairment identified, or students who are still developing these skills. Collecting information about individual students' receptive and expressive language development can be helpful with making modifications to whole-group and small-group instruction.

Chart 1.5 can help build awareness of contributing factors of both receptive and expressive language.

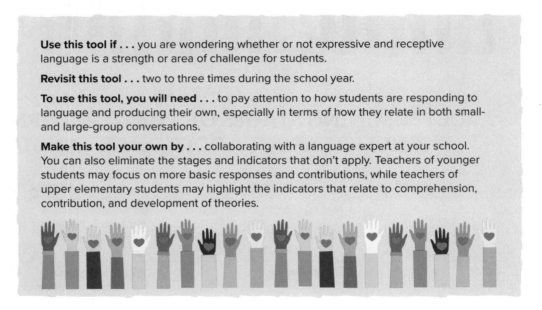

Use this tool if . . . you are wondering whether or not expressive and receptive language is a strength or area of challenge for students.

Revisit this tool . . . two to three times during the school year.

To use this tool, you will need . . . to pay attention to how students are responding to language and producing their own, especially in terms of how they relate in both small- and large-group conversations.

Make this tool your own by . . . collaborating with a language expert at your school. You can also eliminate the stages and indicators that don't apply. Teachers of younger students may focus on more basic responses and contributions, while teachers of upper elementary students may highlight the indicators that relate to comprehension, contribution, and development of theories.

CHART 1.5
COLLECTING INFORMATION ABOUT SPEECH AND LANGUAGE DEVELOPMENT

SPEECH AND LANGUAGE: JANUARY 2020			
	Consistently	Sometimes	Not Yet
Receptive Language			
Follows directions	Kierra, Charlie, Alex, Thomas, Michael, Sanara, Kathleen, Manu, Kendra, Olivia, Sophia, Sanique	Seth, Mara, TJ, Kyron, Amar, Rashad,	Dean
Understands questions	Kierra, Charlie, Alex, Thomas, Michael, Sanara, Kathleen, Manu, Kendra, Olivia, Sophia, Sanique, Seth, Mara	Kyron, Amar, Rashad	Dean, TJ

SPEECH AND LANGUAGE: JANUARY 2020			
	Consistently	Sometimes	Not Yet
Understands stories/read alouds	Kierra, Charlie, Alex, Thomas, Michael, Sanara, Kathleen, Manu, Kendra, Olivia, Sophia, Sanique, Seth, Mara, Kyron	Amar, Rashad	Dean, TJ, Seth
Understands vocabulary	Kierra, Charlie, Alex, Thomas, Michael, Sanara, Kathleen, Manu, Kendra, Olivia, Sophia, Sanique, Mara, Kyron	Amar, Rashad	Dean, TJ, Seth
Expressive Language			
Responds to questions	Kierra, Charlie, Alex, Thomas, Michael, Sanara, Kathleen, Kyron, Kendra, Olivia, Sophia, Sanique	Seth, Mara, TJ, Amar, Rashad, Manu	Dean
Tells stories	Kierra, Charlie, Alex, Thomas, Michael, Sanara, Kathleen, Manu, Kendra, Olivia, Sophia, Sanique, Mara	Kyron, Amar, Rashad, Seth	Dean, TJ
Expresses feelings	Kierra, Charlie, Alex, Thomas, Michael, Sanara, Kathleen, Manu, Kendra, Olivia, Sophia, Sanique, Seth, Mara, Kyron	Amar, Rashad	Dean, TJ, Seth
Participates and extends conversations	Kierra, Charlie, Alex, Thomas, Michael, Sanara, Kathleen, Manu, Kendra, Olivia, Sophia, Sanique, Mara, Kyron	Amar, Rashad	Dean, TJ, Seth
Uses correct syntax	Kierra, Charlie, Alex, Thomas, Michael, Sanara, Kathleen, Manu, Kendra, Olivia, Sophia, Sanique, Mara, Kyron	Amar, Rashad, Sanara	Dean, TJ, Seth
Uses and develops vocabulary	Kierra, Charlie, Alex, Thomas, Michael, Kathleen, Manu, Kendra, Olivia, Sophia, Sanique, Mara, Kyron	Amar, Rashad, Sanara	Dean, TJ, Seth

online resources Available for download at **resources.corwin.com/responsivewritingteacher.**

COLLECTING INFORMATION FOR CULTURAL RESPONSIVENESS

Cultural
Responsiveness
↓

Collect information
about . . .

The cultural and social
identities of students

The Distant Drum
By Calvin C. Hernton, social critic, poet, novelist 1932–2001

I am not a metaphor or symbol.
This you hear is not the wind in the trees,
Nor a cat being maimed in the street.
I am being maimed in the street.
It is I who weep, laugh, feel pain or joy,
Speak this because I exist.
This is my voice.
These words are my words,
My mouth speaks theme,
My hand writes—
I am a poet.
It is my fist you hear
Beating against your ear.

In June 2020, more than ten thousand educators joined the virtual KidLit4BlackLives rally, organized by Kwame Alexander, Jason Reynolds, and Jacqueline Woodson and hosted by the Brown Bookshelf.

In his segment, Jason Reynolds read the poem "The Distant Drum" (Hernton, n.d.) and explained, "This is not a poem about violence. This is a poem about how we use art, how we use other mechanisms to express ourselves, how we use protests, dance and song, how we use our voices, our bodies."

Writing, in its many modalities, is a vessel for liberation—a sanctuary for children to see and be seen, to listen to their inner voice and speak truth, to remember and heal, to explore and teach, to escape and create, to process and feel. But liberation cannot exist without validation. It is within what is learned about students in this domain, about social and cultural identities, that is the foundation for relationship building, for the trust that bonds writer and reader.

Collecting Information About the Cultural and Social Identities of Students

An environment in which children know their written words are safe and honored begins with a community in which every child is safe and honored. Sara Ahmed (2018) writes the following in *Being the Change*:

> We have an obligation to make kids feel visible. When we recognize and value students' identities, we make time and space for them in the daily classroom routines, curriculum, and dialogue. We can help students shine a light on who

they are: their hopes and dreams, talents, family histories, how they identify culturally, the languages they speak, how they learn best, the story of their names, what they can teach us. (p. 2)

In the beginning of the school year, and throughout, embedding explorations of identity in curriculum serves several purposes: opening space for students to form a stronger sense of self, opening space for a classroom culture of safety and visibility, and opening space for stakeholders to know one another. Ideas for identity exploration continue to expand and increase in modality in schools around the world. We share a glimpse into this inspiring work through identity webs, peer interviews, "I am" poems, self-portraits, and heart maps.

Facing History and Ourselves (n.d.), a website and resource for teaching students about the past in order to create more equity in the future, describes identity webs as tools for considering the many factors that shape who we are not only as individuals but also as community members. Figure 1.6 shows four examples of student identity webs from our classrooms and our colleagues' classrooms.

Figure 1.6 Examples of Student Identity Webs

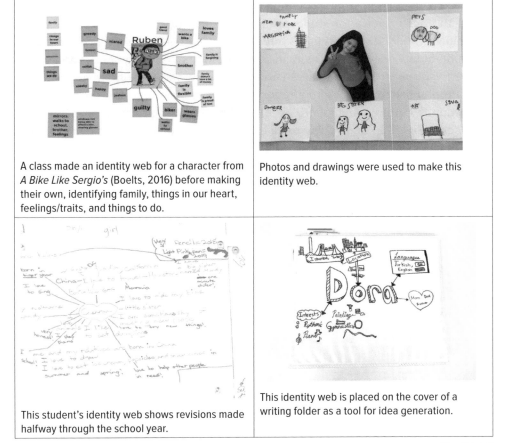

A class made an identity web for a character from *A Bike Like Sergio's* (Boelts, 2016) before making their own, identifying family, things in our heart, feelings/traits, and things to do.

Photos and drawings were used to make this identity web.

This student's identity web shows revisions made halfway through the school year.

This identity web is placed on the cover of a writing folder as a tool for idea generation.

(*Continued*)

(Continued)

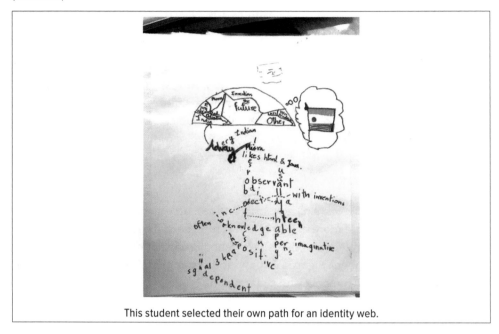

This student selected their own path for an identity web.

In a 2020 podcast from Dr. Sheldon Eakins of the Leading Equity Center, Kelisa Wing offers another exercise for students to explore identity. Wing suggests learning about identities by having students interview each other, looking for commonality: "Have them interview their classmates and get to know the classmates and where they come from and who they are." This activity serves several objectives, including speaking and listening skills; finding common ground; and learning about interests, backgrounds, cultures, and identities—all of which build cultural responsiveness in classrooms. Figure 1.7 shows classroom examples and tools developed by teachers at Kelsey's school.

Figure 1.7 Example of Identity Interviews

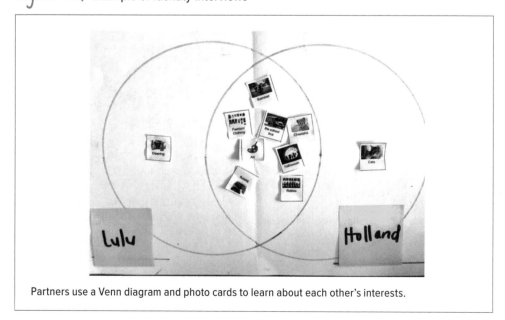

Partners use a Venn diagram and photo cards to learn about each other's interests.

Chestnut Bingo!

My Name: _____ Date: _____

Mingle around the classroom. Use **hand up, pair up** to find a friend. Ask your friend some questions to get to know more about them! Have your friend sign your Bingo card in a box that describes them!

I have a pet!	I play a sport!	I have a sibling.	I like pizza!	I like to cook!
I like to play outside!	Visual arts is my favorite special!	I walk to school.	My birthday is in the summer.	Music is my favorite special!
Sustainability is my favorite special!	My birthday is in the winter.	I am a Chestnut! Your name: _____	I love to read fiction!	I like to play in the rain!
I ride the bus to school!	I eat ice cream!	My birthday is in the spring!	I like swimming in the ocean!	My birthday is in the fall!
I love to read non-fiction!	I like to eat spinach!	I can whistle!	I like to rest in the cozy corner!	I would like to travel to Alaska!

Find someone who...

does not drink coffee.	has more than one kid at Compass.	grew up in NYC.	spends lots of time in Fort Greene Park.	helps deliver or take care of new babies.
has a child under the age of two.	does not eat meat.	bikes in NYC.	grows food in NYC.	has a child over the age of 10.
designs or makes clothing or accessories.	sends their child to Kids Orbit.	has a pet(s) at home.	is an artist (or works at an art museum).	has a child who takes the school bus to or from school.
has been to a Family School Collaborative (FSC) meeting.	grew up in the United States (but not in NYC).	can do hair, nails, and/or makeup.	knows how to use a sewing machine.	grew up outside of the United States.
knows a lot about constructing, fixing, or designing buildings.	has a big family.	has twins in their family.	is raising a bilingual or multilingual child.	uses math at work.

A bingo board used by the Chestnut class to learn about each other's identity

A bingo board used at an open house for families of a class

"Where I'm From," by George Ella Lyon (n.d.), "February 12, 1963," by Jacqueline Woodson (2014), and "Where You From?" by Reneé Watson (2020), can become mentors for students to write their own identity poems. Figure 1.8 shows some examples of students' identity poems. There are many more ways for students to explore and portray their identities by using visual art, such as self-portraits, name meaning drawings, heart maps, identity border drawings, and multilingual art; examples of each are shown in Figure 1.9.

Figure 1.8 Examples of Student Identity Poems

An "I am" wall invites responses from students and caregivers.

Students add an "I am not" to their "I am" statements.

(Continued)

(Continued)

"I am" poems are displayed with family photos alongside a world map.

An "I am" poem is placed alongside a self-portrait.

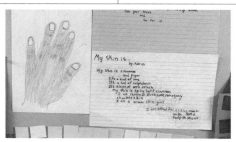

This version of an "I am from" poem focuses on skin color.

Figure 1.9 Examples of Students' Identity Artwork

Self-portraits offer students explicit practice at drawing themselves, which supports them with illustrations in their writing.

Students create lapbooks to show aspects of their identity of choice. This student incorporates multilingual writing to teach about the Chinese Lantern Festival.

This self-portrait includes aspects of student identities.

These self-portraits include student descriptions of skin color.

Students can share name meanings or stories of how they were named.

Heart maps, inspired by Georgia Heard, show family identities.

An identity border creates this self-portrait.

Students can incorporate multilingualism in identity work.

Building Connections With Caregivers

Caregivers and family members are another vital resource for learning about student identities. Some information may already be gathered by school administrators in the beginning of the year. To build upon this, consider the major social indicators: race, language and dialect, family structure, gender, religion, ability, class, and nationality.

While speaking at the KidLit4BlackLives rally, Jason Reynolds urged educators, when working with children and families, to do the following:

Crawl toward judgment, sprint toward understanding . . .

Crawl toward judgment, and sprint toward understanding . . .

Learning about children's lives—through observations, gatherings, surveys, or conversations—requires conscious and deliberate effort to not make assumptions, conclusions, or opinions about people. Doing so is especially important for avoiding implicit biases, or understandings shaped subconsciously by stereotypes. Information collection, in the cultural responsiveness domain (and in all domains), must be done with explicit intention and purpose of seeking understanding.

To connect with families, teachers have used electronic or paper surveys, held listening conferences, visited families at a location selected by each family, made phone calls, or performed a combination of methods, given what is best for each family. Family participation is ideal, but students can help with answering the questions in special circumstances.

When planning questions to ask caregivers, begin with open-ended questions. Then ask more specific questions (if time) and save any logistical questions or messages for last. For any in-person visit with families, such as listening conferences, set the tone for a safe and collaborative conversation. Here are many possible questions, curated by the founding staff of Compass Charter School, which can be customized or selected based on the needs of each student and caregiver in mind. It's not recommended to use all of these questions; instead, choose several that are most relevant from each category.

Setting the Tone (if meeting in person):

- Create a seating arrangement that encourages a conversation: perhaps placing chairs in an open space, or sitting next to family members.
- Have snacks and water available.
- Be open about taking notes during the conference.
- Restate the purpose of the meeting clearly in order to clarify why teachers take notes.

Examples of Open-Ended Questions (start with what feels most appropriate):

- What are your hopes and dreams for your child this year?
- How are you feeling about the start of the school year?
- What do you want us to know about your child?
- What are your child's interests?
- What are your child's likes and dislikes?
- What are your child's strengths? Challenges?

Examples of More Specific Questions (consider asking if time allows):

- What do you and your child enjoy doing together?
- Does your child have siblings? Do you want us to know anything about their sibling relationships?
- How was your summer?
- What are your favorite memories of school?
- Have there been any recent changes in your child's life?

- Do any members of your family have special hobbies, interests, or areas of expertise that they would be willing to share to enrich our inquiry and play?
- Is there anything we can do or should know to help your child have a smooth transition into this classroom?
- What is your child's preferred setting for playing or working (i.e., location, group size, position—sitting, standing, lying)?
- What are some important parts of your family's identity? Can you recommend a special book that your family or child identifies with or that will help the class get to know them? Parts of your family's identity may include, but are not limited to, race, ethnicity, religion, language, family structure, family traditions, family history, favorite foods, and pastimes; where you live or have lived before; strengths and challenges; or anything else that feels like an important part of who you are (and that you feel comfortable sharing with us).

Examples of Logistical Questions:

- Does your child have a preferred name, nickname, or pronoun?
- If a family expresses interest in volunteer opportunities . . .
- How would you like to get involved in supporting the classroom or school?
- How would you like us to contact and correspond with you (email, phone call, text, in person)?
- When is it best to reach you?
- Invite families to send in or email photos with their child.

Closure:

- Do you have any questions? (Allow time for potential questions from the family.)

Chart 1.6 is an example of a tool that can be used to learn more about student and family identity during meetings with caregivers.

Use this tool if . . . you meet with caregivers or send surveys at the beginning of the year.

Revisit this tool . . . at the beginning of new units as you are planning ways to reflect and build upon student identities.

To use this tool, you will need . . . to determine the best way to collect information. For example, what language(s) will it need to be translated into for your students' families to participate? What is the most accessible way for families to share this information?

Make this tool your own by . . . deciding what information is most relevant to your students and curriculum. Keep in mind that caregivers may feel overwhelmed by a long questionnaire, so you may want to limit it to five or six questions.

CHART 1.6

COLLECTING INFORMATION FROM CAREGIVERS

STUDENT NAME	CAREGIVER NAME(S)	NOTES
Lillie	*Nora, Jen, Maggie* (birth mom), *Christine* (sister)	Excited to take the bus to school Has seasonal allergies: uses an inhaler Likes to help and do his own thing Loves to dance, sing, eat, run, dress up in costumes; dramatic play Learning how to skateboard Has two moms, both siblings adopted—knows about this and is in touch with birth mom Hopes and dreams: for her to be happy and to learn as much as possible
Mateo	*Dayana, George*	Oldest of siblings, has two half siblings Switches between homes each week: this is a new transition Speaks Spanish, Swedish, and English, more fluent in Spanish—speaks Spanish primarily at home Likes to be the leader in environments Makes up answers if not sure what they are Energetic: bikes or runs to school Likes to look at books, encyclopedia books, dinosaurs, soccer, planes, trains Loves to sing; taking violin lessons Wants him to ask questions, to love school Wants to make sure he eats every day
Ruby	*Merrie, Lee*	Smart, sharp, attentive, observant, stubborn Black child in a predominantly white family Loves the natural world, scientific inquiry, excellent observer; loves animals Takes gymnastics Loves dance and music; loves to watch music videos Talks about race; family has built networks including many Black families Hopes and dreams: to be happy about being a learner

online resources ↖ Available for download at **resources.corwin.com/responsivewritingteacher.**

It may be helpful to organize information gathered about student identities in one place, for future referencing when planning. Chart 1.7 provides an outline for doing so.

Use this tool if . . . you've gathered cultural information about individual students and are ready to reflect upon and access data across the classroom.

Revisit this tool . . . at the beginning of new units as you are planning ways to reflect and represent student identities in curriculum.

To use this tool, you will need . . . information collected from Chart 1.6 or a similar tool.

Make this tool your own by . . . changing the considerations we included. Decide what aspects of your students' cultures and identities are most relevant.

CHART 1.7

CLASSROOM IDENTITIES AT A GLANCE

	Classroom Representations
Languages	French
	Spanish
	Arabic
	Japanese
Race and nationalities	Black — Haitian
	Japanese — Jamaican
	Spanish
	Dutch, Swedish
	Arabic
Neighborhoods populated, former places lived	Florida
	Jamaica
	Upstate
	Spain (summer)
	Japan
Family structures	Transitions between homes
	Single Caregiver
	Two dads
	^

online resources Available for download at **resources.corwin.com/responsivewritingteacher**.

COLLECTING INFORMATION FOR SOCIAL-EMOTIONAL RESPONSIVENESS

Social-Emotional Responsiveness
↓
Collect information about . . .
Student interests within and outside of school
The social-emotional tendencies of students in relation to writing

"I remember things about students from twenty years ago."

For Jana, a third-grade teacher, getting to know her students is of highest priority in the first weeks of the school year, and she gathers information across the day. Jana sits at the door as her class unpacks, taking the time to check in with each student. During morning choice time, Jana circulates the room, talking to each student about their work. While becoming familiar with the new classroom environment, students draw things they love on blank borders, which become frames for bulletin boards. Jana takes notes during morning meeting each day, recording answers from students to daily questions and shares. Caregivers are asked to share a message about their child, to help Jana get to know them. Students compile collages on composition notebooks with words and images that portray their identity. Writing begins with a personal narrative study, and four or five writers share each day. Jana explains:

I find something about each child to incorporate in classroom conversations, demonstrations, examples, and connections throughout the school year. As kids get older, I think it becomes less important to love a teacher and more important to feel connected to a teacher. My hope is, by frequently naming things that kids identify with, they feel seen, and if I show genuine interest, they feel connected. Then, this seeing and naming and showing interest happens between students— that's what bonds us as a community.

Collecting Information About Student Interests

Responsive educators pay attention to body language and listen to students, talking with them throughout the day, throughout the year. This attention means learning *about* students and *from* them—about their lives, their strengths, their struggles, what matters to them. And all of it matters to both instruction and learning.

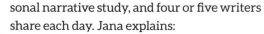

Adapting writing tasks so that they align with student interests contributes to a stimulating writing environment and positively affects the quality of student writing (Graham & Harris, 2016). Within areas of interest for children emerge seeds for writing, conversations, and connections between students. Donald Graves (1985/2020) wrote this: "All children have important experiences and interests they can learn to tap through writing. If children are to become independent learners, we have to help them know what they know; this process begins with helping children to choose their own topics."

We can learn and take note of the interests of students in many ways:

- Asking caregivers and family members
- Observing play in the classroom and outdoors
- Listening to topics shared in class meetings
- Studying the topics of books students read
- Joining lunch or snack conversations
- Looking at what students draw or engage in during choice times throughout the day
- Asking students directly!

Tip for Tomorrow

Sara Ahmed (2018), in *Being the Change*, inspires teachers to think about students in terms of nouns and verbs, as opposed to adjectives. Similarly, Julie Wright and Barry Hoonan (2018) emphasize kidwatching in *What Are You Grouping For?* What do we really know about our students in terms of what *matters* to them and what they *do?* Can we do more than describe the levels of students? One exercise that can be insightful for guiding kidwatching, relationship building, and dialogue is to create a chart of student names with nouns and verbs as column headers. See how much you can fill in about students.

Chart 1.8 can be used to gather information about student interests. This tool is structured around a goal of knowing (at least) three areas of interest for each child.

Use this tool if . . . you are learning what students are interested in.

Revisit this tool . . . as you learn new interests about children, or before new genre studies, to narrow the scope of what they are interested in.

To use this tool, you will need . . . to talk to children about what they are interested in, observe them in play, or ask their caregivers.

Make this tool your own by . . . adding specific activities that you know are important to students in your classroom, as we have not captured all of the categories of interests that exist across classrooms.

CHART 1.8

COLLECTING INFORMATION ABOUT STUDENT INTERESTS

STUDENTS (List all students in your classroom; use multiple sheets if necessary.)	INTERESTS		
	Notice: books read, topics of writing, topics of drawings, topics of conversations, choices at playtime or recess **Might include:** family members, pets, animals, music, TV shows or movies, sports, hobbies, places, toys, family traditions, holidays		
Charlie	Surfing	Dog: Winnie Sister: Kate LOVES cousin	Big into exercise, healthy eating
Mara	Reading, baking	Only child No pets	Jewish: loves her camp, planning bar mitzvah, creating a book drive
Seth	Baseball, soccer	Loves snakes	Wants to be a doctor
Amar	Cooks with Ama every night	Writes and reads comics	Plays Minecraft with sisters
Dean	Harry Potter: currently reading with his dads each night	Climbing: goes to rock climbing classes	Playing dress-up and pretend
Kierra	Making DIY videos—especially of slime, constructions, art projects	Likes cats and bears—doesn't have pets but loves them; knows every dog in her building and keeps treats for them	Wants to own her own salon—does face painting and nails and hair with neighbors already
TJ	Music, dancing, hip-hop; aunt is DJ	Collections: nature, loose parts, keeps in suitcase	Wants to get better at playing basketball so that he can play with big brother and sister
Rashad	Ninjago with cousins	Sharks! Once caught one while fishing	Learned how to surf over the summer Competes in gymnastics
Olivia	Skateboarding	Cooking: her mom is a chef	Sings, writes songs, and plays ukulele
Sophia	Loves Rocky, her puppy Talks about baby sister and brother often	Wants to be an astronaut and knows all about space and Mae Jemison	Makes art from reusable materials Always has a plan

online resources ↖ Available for download at **resources.corwin.com/responsivewritingteacher.**

Collecting Information About Social-Emotional Habits of Students in Relation to Writing

Because we are teacher-writers (and we hope you are a teacher who writes as well!—more to come on that in Chapter 5), we know writing is not an easy task. Writers encounter all kinds of challenges—a block in ideas, difficulty staying on task, frustration when unsatisfied with work—we've experienced them all! And students do too.

Having the ability to persist and persevere through challenges is essential in the writing process. Just as we have our own capacities of stamina, tolerance for frustration, and flexibility, students also arrive in classrooms with their own. The more students' emotional tendencies are understood, appreciated, and supported—as writers and as learners across content areas—the more prepared they can be for a lifetime of learning.

Chart 1.9 can be used when collecting information about the habits of minds at play as students approach a writing task. These competencies wax and wane depending on the experiences of writers, and it's important to think about the frame of minds of writers. Do they believe they can or can't? Leaning on the research of Carol Dweck (2006) around growth mindset, Mraz and Hertz (2015) offer five research-driven attitudes, and these attitudes include the following:

- Empathy
- Flexibility
- Resiliency
- Optimism
- Persistence

When students develop positive learning mindsets, their motivation increases. In turn, when students' motivation to study, learn, and build academic skills increases, they are better prepared to learn and perform in the future (Quay & Romero, 2015). As always, incorporate any additional habits of mind that are applicable in your own classroom.

Use this tool if . . . you are integrating social-emotional learning in your curriculum. Gathering information about the habits of mind of your students will help you decide which skills individual students or the majority of students can grow—as writers and beyond.

Revisit this tool . . . several times each year. Information collected using this tool can be helpful to share in progress reports or for parent-teacher conferences.

To use this tool, you will need . . . to observe students during independent writing time and note their behaviors during conferences and partner or group share time.

Make this tool your own by . . . modifying the behaviors or indicators to be more representative of your students and grade level.

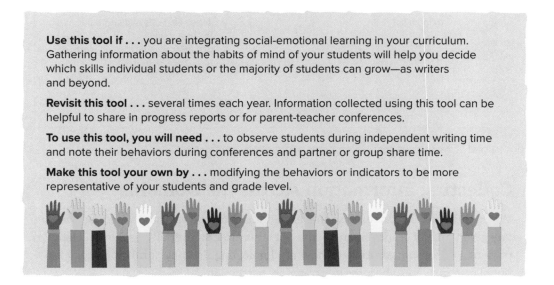

CHART 1.9

COLLECTING INFORMATION ABOUT WRITERLY HABITS OF MIND

Genre of Writing/Unit of Study: _____ Opinion _____

STUDENTS	TRAIT	INDICATORS IN WRITING
Strength for: Kierra, Charlie, Alex, Thomas, Michael, Seth, Mara, Kate, Sanara, Rashad, Kathleen, Olivia, Sophia, Sanique Goal for: Amar, Dean, Kyron, TJ, Manu, Kendra	Perseverance	• Maintains stamina • Continues writing when the idea or skill is challenging • Continues practicing the strategy after receiving support
Strength for: Kierra, Dean, Charlie, Alex, Thomas, Michael, Seth, Mara, Kate, Sanara, Rashad, Kathleen, Olivia, Sophia, Sanique, Amar, TJ, Kendra, Manu Goal for: Kyron	Empathy	• Offers helpful feedback to others • Notices when peers need help and offers it • Includes feelings in pictures and words
Strength for: Kierra, Charlie, Alex, Thomas, Michael, Seth, Mara, Kate, Sanara, Rashad, Kathleen, Olivia, Sophia, Sanique, Manu, Kendra, Amar Goal for: Dean, Kyron, TJ	Resilience	• When attempting a skill or strategy without success, tries again • Begins again after being unhappy with what was written
Strength for: Charlie, Alex, Thomas, Michael, Seth, Mara, Kate, Sanara, Rashad, Kathleen, Olivia, Sophia, Sanique, Manu, Kendra, Amar Goal for: Dean, Kyron, TJ, Kierra	Flexibility	• Tries spelling multiple ways when unsure • Makes revisions in writing • Is open to feedback
Strength for: Kierra, Charlie, Alex, Thomas, Michael, Seth, Mara, Kate, Sanara, Rashad, Kathleen, Olivia, Sophia, Sanique, Manu, Kendra, Amar Goal for: Dean, Kyron, TJ	Optimism	• Tries new skills and strategies independently • Attempts to spell difficult words or write long sentences

online resources Available for download at **resources.corwin.com/responsivewritingteacher.**

Collecting Information Across the Domains

While this book is structured so that each domain can be revisited when focusing on any given area of responsiveness, the domains are not mutually exclusive. Here we present a classroom example of how academic, linguistic, cultural, and social-emotional responsiveness become integrated in instruction.

Putting it in Practice

If you had looked at Rose's writing in the winter, you might have noticed she was not yet approaching grade-level expectations. Rose receives occupational therapy, and the physicality of writing posed many barriers on her development. It was challenging for Rose to organize pictures and words on paper in a way that was legible for readers. On paper, it did not appear that Rose had formed the concept of words versus letters. Rose's stamina and volume fell short of her peers.

What you would not have seen on paper is that Rose is a proud big sister of George, who she is utterly enamored with. You would not have heard her speak three languages: English, French, and Japanese. You could not have seen that her room is filled with toy figurines or that she carefully chooses several to carry in her backpack each day. Rose's uncertainty in new environments does not show on paper, nor does her desire to stay close to who she is comfortable with. Luckily, Rose's teacher knew these things—from looking at pictures shared by her grown-ups, from listening to stories shared during the morning meeting, from close observations at playtime and snack time. Rose's teacher knew Rose as a learner *and as a human* and used all that she knew to help Rose grow into a confident writer.

At playtime, Rose's occupational therapist provided Rose with space to draw maps for her figurines. During writing, it helped Rose to feel and look closely at figurines before drawing them. Rose's teacher coached Rose at the beginning of independent time, providing encouragement and support before working alone. Rose wrote near friends, who offered a sense of comfort. After a few weeks of writing about figurines, Rose became confident to write about more topics: making cake, picking apples, and examining animal life cycles. Rose's stamina grew as well. By the end of the school year, Rose met writing benchmarks. What cannot show on the data that will travel with her to first grade, however, is the joy Rose now has as a writer and reader of books.

Digging Deeper

Throughout the chapter, we referenced specific resources. To read more about any of these concepts, we recommend the following books:

- *Kidwatching: Documenting Children's Literacy Development* by Gretchen Owocki and Yetta Goodman (2002)

- *What Are You Grouping For? Grades 3–8: How to Guide Small Groups Based on Readers—Not the Book* by Julie Wright and Barry Hoonan (2018)

- *A Mindset for Learning: Teaching the Traits of Joyful, Independent Growth* by Kristine Mraz and Christine Hertz (2015)

- *Mindset: The New Psychology of Success* by Carol Dweck (2006)

- *Culturally Responsive Teaching and The Brain: Promoting Authentic Engagement and Rigor Among Culturally and Linguistically Diverse Students* by Zaretta Hammond (2015)

- *Heart Maps: Helping Students Craft Authentic Writing* by Georgia Heard (2016)

- *Linguistic Justice: Black Language, Literacy, Identity, and Pedagogy* by April Baker-Bell (2020)

Tool for Planning Across the Domains

Collecting Information

This tool can be used as a place to take notes, reflect, or expand upon the ideas in this chapter. Alternatively, it can also be used to plan for responsiveness across the domains.

Academic Responsiveness • *Content-related skills* • *Writing-related behaviors and processes*	**Linguistic Responsiveness** • *Home language(s)* • *Speaking and processing skills* • *Language and vocabulary development*
Cultural Responsiveness • *Cultural and social identities*	**Social-Emotional Responsiveness** • *Interests* • *Social-emotional tendencies*

online resources Available for download at **resources.corwin.com/responsivewritingteacher.**

CHAPTER 2

Planning Responsive Instruction

Responsive plans are made from a place of knowing. No curriculum writer, no plan maker knows the writers in a classroom like the teacher does. A responsive writing teacher crafts instruction that aligns with students' developing skills, languages, identities, and interests.

"Do you think our tree house will still be there?"

The class hurried into the forest on a weekly trip to the neighborhood park. On a previous visit, they discovered several large branches, which became a climbing apparatus.

Ecstatic to see the large branches still rested upon the tree trunk, a line quickly formed. A parent volunteer stayed with the line of children, coaching and offering a boost when needed. This was the most supported climb up.

Other children, who were more experienced climbers, ventured off to another patch of trees, where they wrapped their legs around the trunk and shimmied up without help.

Several kids found new falling logs and rested them up against the tallest tree yet. For the most difficult and risky climb, a short line formed, supported by the classroom teacher. Two students made it up, immediately cheered on by the class.

Everyone who had set a goal to climb a tree found success this day, with agency in determining the just-right path. In the weeks that followed, tree climbing remained an activity of high interest, with children challenging themselves in a progression of increments, growing more and more independent with each attempt.

Why Responsive Plans Matter

In a 2018 interview, Zaretta Hammond stated, "Engagement comes when we are doing complex cognitive work that is fun… it is all about helping students not only reclaim their sense of confidence but be the leaders of their own learning—getting them to the point where as independent learners they are carrying the majority of the cognitive load."

The learning environment of our dreams looks like the forest did that day: kids motivated by highly engaging goals, who are invited to practice through multiple paths of entry, in an atmosphere of trusted peer collaboration and feedback, with safe grounds for taking risks—alongside teachers, who coach, nudge, and offer a boost when needed.

Such an environment *is* possible, though it cannot be preprescribed. There is not *one* plan that we nor anyone else can offer that leads to the energy described. Such a plan can only be crafted for the classroom in which it will come to life. This is not to say educators should abandon curricular plans or devise their plans from scratch. These plans anchor work in developmental benchmarks, norm learning experiences across grade levels, and are often based on researched methods of learning.

What we are suggesting, and hope to make actionable in this chapter, is that educators modify, or as Cornelius Minor (2018) describes in *We Got This,* bend curriculum to align with each group of writers: the strengths, goals, language development, cultures, and interests that cannot be predicted by curriculum writers.

Types of Plans

Thinking about plans, we funnel our considerations into the ideas and concepts students should learn for the year, how those concepts divide and support units of study, and then the daily teaching and learning plans that take aim at key standards and learning objectives. Many districts have a scope and sequence that structure and guide the year of learning. From there, units exist, outlining what students should be able to do and understand at various points.

The Understanding By Design framework, as described by Grant Wiggins and Jay McTighe (2011), aligns standards and content in three stages:

- Stage 1: Identify desired results.
- Stage 2: Determine assessment evidence.
- Stage 3: Plan learning experiences and instruction.

Leaning on this framework, begin by determining the concepts and skills students should learn by the end of the year; many districts have a scope and sequence that structures and guides the year of learning. From there, unit plans or genre studies provide a context for the instruction of those concepts and skills. At that point, daily plans can be designed with specific learning objectives. These plans contain opportunities for the following:

- A short lesson with a clearly defined teaching point
- Small-group lessons that target specific skills
- Individual conferences with students
- Share sessions when student work can be highlighted

Planning Across the Domains

Knowing students across all four domains is a prerequisite to the responsive modifications in this chapter (and in each chapter that follows!). The planning tools provided work best alongside information collected, which is why we reference Chapter 1 so frequently.

In our opinion, this work is among the most challenging aspects of writing instruction. It can be, without a doubt, disheartening when carefully designed plans don't result in targeted growth. When this happens, the focus is often this: Why aren't students progressing as they *should* be? Responsive instruction reframes this question: Why aren't plans leading to targeted growth for students?

While writing this book, we wondered how to modify plans to better fit students (rather than the other way around). We even experimented with trying different approaches, paying close attention to the impact we have on student learning. Action research is powerful, and we leaned on the four-step model of identifying a problem or question, planning an approach, collecting data, and then analyzing or deciding upon next steps (Sagor, 2011). This approach inspired us to consider and then plan for various entry points and domains, capitalizing on students' strengths and supporting them in their development and learning.

As Myles Horton and Paulo Freire (1990) illustrate in *We Make the Road by Walking: Conversations on Education and Social Change,*

> The teacher is of course an artist, but being an artist does not mean that [they] can make the profile, can shape the students. What the educator does in teaching is to make it possible for students to become themselves.

Through multiple entry points, accessible language, representative contexts, and topics of interest, teachers can lean on what is known about students to plan instruction with as much emphasis on liberation as on academic skills.

Academic Responsiveness ↓	Linguistic Responsiveness ↓	Cultural Responsiveness ↓	Social-Emotional Responsiveness ↓
Plan instruction that has . . .			
Multiple entry points for students to access instruction and develop skills Differentiated systems and structures for students to access instruction and practice independently	Supports to help students understand, communicate, and develop content-specific language and vocabulary Supports for students who are developing expressive and receptive language	Connections, content, and contexts that are reflective of diverse communities	Writing experiences that are meaningful and align with student interests Safe and supportive opportunities for students to take risks and work collaboratively

ACADEMICALLY RESPONSIVE PLANNING

Academic Responsiveness ↓
Plan instruction that has . . .
Multiple entry points for students to access instruction and develop skills
Differentiated systems and structures for students to access instruction and practice independently

Bounce. Swish. "YEAH!" Kelsey looked out of her window and waved to her downstairs neighbor, Jayden, and his friend Mila. For two weeks, Mila and Jayden have been attempting an alley-oop—watching videos of professionals, breaking down the steps, and getting coached by Mila's dad. Upon a successful pass and dunk, the friends leaped around the yard

in hard-earned jubilation. From our earliest years to adulthood, it's in human nature to feel good upon learning something new. In *Culturally Responsive Teaching and The Brain*, Hammond (2015) explains that dopamine—a neurotransmitter and hormone associated with pleasure and learning—is released in brains when humans experience success.

Jayden and Mila may not have experienced this triumph, or been so motivated to practice, had they been attempting an alley-oop on a regulated basketball hoop. Jayden's backyard hoop had been lowered to a height within reach, upon the goal they set. Such a setup made the alley-oop and environment for practice within Mila and Jayden's zone of proximal development (ZPD). Lev Vygotsky (1978) described the ZPD as the area within a task where learners can be independent with some guidance, support, or scaffolding but will become independent in the near future (see Figure 2.1). When lessons and tasks are within learners' ZPDs, they have the greatest impact on learning rates and on students' beliefs in themselves as capable learners.

Figure 2.1 If instruction happens within the band of the ZPD, then learners need some guidance or scaffolding but not so much that they feel overwhelmed by the new concepts.

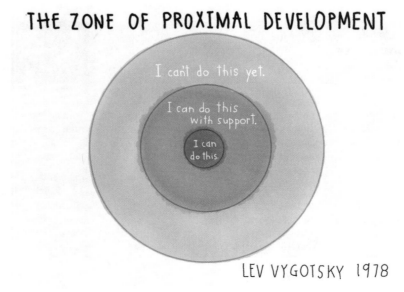

THE ZONE OF PROXIMAL DEVELOPMENT

I can't do this yet.

I can do this with support.

I can do this.

LEV VYGOTSKY 1978

Planning Multiple Entry Points for Students to Access Information and Develop Skills

Academically responsive planning involves finding ways to support students that neither underestimates their competency and potential nor oversupports in a way that renders independence impossible. In her 1995 article about culturally responsive teaching, Gloria Ladson-Billings emphasized the importance of students feeling like they are empowered. "When we know we're getting better at something, we will lean into it more," Zaretta Hammond stated in an interview with instructional coach Jim Knight (2018).

One way to set students up for success and empowerment is to plan for multiple *entry points* for developing a skill. An entry point can be described as the place in which a writer can assimilate instruction and make sense of it, based on understanding and knowledge from previous instruction and experiences. In the introduction, the trees were like entry points, providing a range of opportunities for children to practice climbing, based on prior experience. As Cornelius Minor (2018) explains in *We Got This*, "We cannot guarantee outcomes, but we can guarantee access. We can ensure that everyone gets a shot."

When planning for a range of entry points, think about different techniques and strategies students can use to develop a skill. For example, students can develop the skill of *including dialogue* multiple ways: speech bubbles, use of quotation marks and dialogue tags, and with back-and-forth conversations. Students can also use the support of technology to record dialogue of characters on a book-writing app. These strategies for dialogue incorporation offer different entry points depending on preexisting skills and readiness.

Chart 2.1 can be used for thinking about targeted skills and planning different entry points that respond to varying needs of students.

Use this tool if . . . you are making differentiated plans based on the skills students are developing.

Revisit this tool . . . throughout a unit. It can be a constant source of information for high-impact small-group work because it nudges the consideration of what students need to know in order to make progress.

To use this tool, you will need . . . to reference academic information collected (see Chapter 1) and look at student writing routinely.

Make this tool your own by . . . adding goals that most closely match the goals of students and are aligned with any curricular or school-wide goals.

CHART 2.1
PLANNING ENTRY POINTS FOR SKILLS

Primary-Grade Example

STUDENTS	SKILL TO WORK ON	POSSIBLE ENTRY POINTS FOR TECHNIQUES AND STRATEGIES
Samar **Lilly** **Ben** **Oliver**	Naming and writing about a topic	Idea-generation tools: Print photos shared by families/taken in the classroom of interests Make chart: Writers get ideas from . . . • Things we do • Thinks we like • Things that are important
Kathleen **Macca** **Lily**	Organizing an idea across pages	Oral rehearsal plan across fingers: kids can trace their hand in folder as a visual/kinesthetic tool for this. Ideas can be sketched on each page on a sticky note, then stuck on each page before writing to aid with memory
Kim **Olivia** **Josh**	Drawing clear pictures	Small- or large-group interactive drawing: Mentor text, labeled elements of clear pictures Chart to show details: writers show shape, color, size, texture
Jacob **Sofia** **Mara** **Abby** **Ben**	Using phonological awareness to write words	Alphabet chart Small- or large-group interactive writing Word wall Spelling strategy chart
Claire **Charlie** **Tess** **Drew** **Amar**	Elaborating with more details in pictures and words	Chart to show ways that "Writers can add more!" after studying a mentor text
Jalen **Shameer** **Nate**	Including spaces between words	Small-group or large-group interactive writing Sticky dots or rectangle stamp to show where each word will go

Upper-Elementary Narrative Example

STUDENTS	SKILL TO WORK ON	POSSIBLE ENTRY POINTS FOR TECHNIQUES AND STRATEGIES
Claire Charlie Julia Jack	Establishing a beginning	Strategy chart Ways to begin: • Dialogue • Setting the scene • Right in the moment • Loud noise or sudden action
Olivia Jenna Ava Will	Sustaining a focus	Reminder cards: • What is your story really about? • What is your claim? • What are you teaching about?
Will Victor Malik Ellie	Creating an ending	Strategy chart Ways to end: • Final thought • Lesson learned • Link to the beginning or middle
Wyatt Katrina Allie Tyler Muma Alia	Knowing the beginning, middle, and ending	Paper scaffold (three-page or five-page packet) Planning template with beginning, middle, and end | B	M	E | |---|---|---|
Samara Talik Ashley	Developing (Elaboration strategies)	Strategy chart Tally cards so that students can track when they use elaboration strategies—talk, action, description, inner thinking.
Brandon Wesley Kate Alex	Using conventions	Personal checklists Goal cards

online resources 🔍 Available for download at **resources.corwin.com/responsivewritingteacher.**

Planning Differentiated Instruction

There are also opportunities for academic responsiveness within differentiated instruction and independent practice. Content of lessons can be differentiated for whole-group instruction, small-group instruction, and individual conferences.

To do so, consider the following:

1. How will students access information in instruction?
2. What tools will support students with independent practice?

In Chapter 1, we described various ways to gather information about the challenges students experience within the writing process. Now, consider ways to modify or supplement the *content*, *process*, *product*, and *environment*.

	Possible Barrier	Possible Support
Content **Ask**: *What contexts, language use, or skills might get in the way of student learning?*	Skill or strategy is beyond the ZPD of students.	Preteaching/reteaching lesson to small group Breaking skill or strategy into smaller steps to teach across multiple days Using visuals and demonstrations that are within ZPD
	Vocabulary is unfamiliar to students.	Using visuals Previewing new vocabulary with students
	Connections are not familiar to or do not reflect students' experiences or home language(s), or students do not have contextual background knowledge.	Revising connections to better align with students' experiences Previewing or translating any essential background knowledge (many apps and Google provide voice and text translation) with students before lesson
Process **Ask**: *What parts of the routine or writing process might get in the way of student practice?*	Transitions have multiple steps that are difficult for students to keep track of	Making a chart for students to use that shows each step with visuals
	It is challenging for students to generate ideas or organize ideas across pages.	Making idea-generation tools and organization tools with students and keeping them in writing folders
	The length of writing time is greater than students' stamina.	Taking individualized breaks (i.e., movement, sensory, meditational) that are built into students' schedules
Product **Ask**: *How might the tools offered get in the way of student practice?*	Paper design—number of lines, space between lines, size of picture box, number of pages— does not offer sufficient space for students.	Offering a variety of paper choices or individualized paper choices for students
	Pencils or pens offered are physically challenging to use for students who are still developing fine-motor muscles.	Adding grips to writing utensils or offering shorter/thicker utensils Using assistive technology
Environment **Ask**: *What in the environment might get in the way of student learning and practice?*	Students are experiencing sensory overload usually because of too much noise or visual stimulation.	Using noise-cancelling headphones, quiet areas of the room, scheduled whisper talk times, and no-talk times to minimize sensory overload Using dim fluorescent lights and soft lighting from lamps or natural light from windows
	Seating does not allow for space or movement needed by students.	Offering flexible seating options to students (e.g., standing spot, seat that provides movement, seat that provides sensory input)
	Charts are too far away for students to see.	Providing small copies of charts in student writing folders, or at tables, or available for use at the writing center

online resources ⌐ Available for download at **resources.corwin.com/responsivewritingteacher**.

Chart 2.2 can help with thinking ahead about any possible barriers for student learning and making plans for differentiated support. The following example shows how to plan for predictable barriers in a lesson about supporting opinion, but this example serves as a template or model for any writing genre at any level.

Use this tool if . . . you are planning ways to remove barriers that may get in the way of accessing lessons and instruction within the content, process, product, or environment.

Revisit this tool . . . throughout the unit as barriers change.

To use this tool, you will need . . . to use some of the information from Chapter 1 in order to assess and then plan for the obstacles and barriers that are impacting student learning.

Make this tool your own by . . . focusing on just one or two of the areas as opposed to all four. Additionally, think of each barrier along a progression. How can you plan differentiation that progresses from most support to least support, so that students experience success and independence?

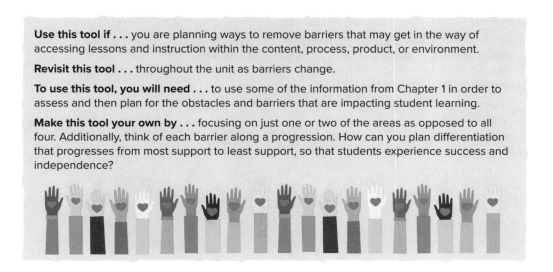

CHART 2.2

PREDICTING BARRIERS AND PLANNING FOR SUPPORT

Focus of lesson: *Writers support an opinion with reasons.*

	CONTENT	PROCESS	PRODUCT	ENVIRONMENT
Possible barrier	Knowing the meaning of opinion and reasons and familiarity with the persuasive genre	Generating ideas	Lines on paper may be too close together	Noise, proximity to peers
Possible methods of differentiation	Previewing vocabulary words during an immersion to genre, before lesson	Creating an idea web prior to lesson or in a small group after lesson	Various paper choices, including blank paper	Noise-cancelling headphones, private writing spot

online resources 🔖 Available for download at **resources.corwin.com/responsivewritingteacher.**

In addition to considering potential barriers, it's also important to plan for the various types of lessons and supports that can happen in classrooms. Depending on the size of the groups, differentiation is possible to a variety of degrees (Sousa & Tomlinson, 2018). Part of the planning process can involve developing and utilizing tools that are specific to the format and size of the group.

Chart 2.3 helps to plan for the supports, access, tools, and opportunities for independent practice that exist across a period of instructional time.

Use this tool if . . . you need to plan scaffolds, modifications, accommodations, or significantly different entry points for whole-group instruction.

Revisit this tool . . . throughout the unit, as you will want to make sure that whatever you have put in place for a student is building independence instead of reinforcing patterns of helplessness.

To use this tool, you will need . . . to have a repertoire of accommodations for access and expression.

Make this tool your own by . . . staying informed of constantly changing and growing options that provide access for students, especially as they relate to technology.

CHART 2.3

PLANNING DIFFERENTIATED SUPPORT

Focus of lesson (or sequence of lessons): Grade 3 Narrative

Date: 9/15/19

	HOW WILL STUDENTS ACCESS INFORMATION IN INSTRUCTION?	WHAT TOOLS WILL SUPPORT STUDENTS WITH INDEPENDENT PRACTICE?
Whole-group supports	Mini lessons offering topic ideas Planning Ways to draft	Charts Paper booklets Exemplar texts Mentor texts Checklists
Small-group supports *List students here:*	Video lessons Small-group lessons	Interactive writing Shared writing Isolated challenges Planning: Michael, Thomas, Lexi Spelling challenges: Cole, Trinity, Madison Getting started: Sanique, Caroline, Max, Cameron
Individual supports	Conferences	Story scaffolds: Marcus, Damien Drawing options: Kate, Max?

LINGUISTICALLY RESPONSIVE PLANNING

Marina Rodriguez, a fourth-grade teacher and coauthor of the *Two Writing Teachers* blog, shared a story about a student who found it challenging to express her thoughts and understand others. This student used an iPad as a classroom communication tool, though upon an immersion in blogging, Marina discovered a new entry point for dialogue between peers:

Linguistic Responsiveness
↓
Plan instruction that has . . .
Supports to help students understand, communicate, and develop content-specific language and vocabulary
Supports for students who are developing expressive and receptive language

> Although she wrote only a few blog posts, she commented over 213 times in response to peer writing within a period of three months. The average number of responses for individual students was fifty out of a group of thirty-four students. Her peers reciprocated and responded. She gained freedom in this environment and her voice gained strength in communicating with others. This experience raised her to a level of equal recognition, attention, and care within her group of peers. It was a freedom she had not experienced before. She came to understand the power of her words and her voice.

The inclusive environment that Marina has cultivated with her students honors and prioritizes all voices and ensures that children are heard—even if (and especially when) it disrupts the norms in which the U.S. school system was built upon.

Planning Supports for Language and Vocabulary Development

With unit or lesson plans accessible, as well as information collected about students' language(s) and linguistic abilities (see Chapter 1), supports can be implemented for content-specific language structures and vocabulary that students will encounter during instruction. At the beginning of a new unit or before a sequence of lessons, ask the following questions:

- What language structures and vocabulary are central to this skill or genre of study?
- What instructional supports will allow students to access, acquire, and use language structures and vocabulary?
- What opportunities are there in instruction and in independent practice to incorporate home languages and/or multilingualism?

Examples of instructional supports might include these:

- Illustrated vocabulary lists or genre-specific word wall
- Sentence frames
- Shared or interactive writing sessions
- Use of mentor or demonstration texts
- Vocabulary or command of language acted out with a partner
- Integration of vocabulary in other content areas or activities
- Translanguaging (inviting students to write in a home language first before translating to English)

Tip for Tomorrow

In *Social Studies for Social Justice,* Rahima Wade (2007) states the following:

A student's home, or native, language is an inseparable part of their identity and culture. It influences how they experience and navigate the world. Though programs that honor heritage languages are becoming more common in the U.S., most schools still provide "English-only" immersion programs with no regard or respect for the continued development of the student's home language. Being literate in two or more languages is an asset for any student, but it's also a way for a student to connect with, understand, and preserve their native culture.

Wade then provides the following list:

How can schools honor students' home languages?

- Take the time to practice and learn the correct pronunciation and spelling of students' names.
- Incorporate words and phrases in students' home language into daily routines: have students share useful words or phrases, and hang them up in the classroom along with English versions.
- Incorporate books, posters, and decor featuring the student's home languages and cultures.
- Allow students to read and write texts in their home languages.
- Create opportunities for students to share stories about their traditions, cultures, languages, and personal experiences.
- Recognize and teach students that African American Vernacular English (AAVE), also known as Black English, or Black Language, is a valid language with grammar rules and structures like any other language, and respect its use by native speakers in the classroom.

Chart 2.4 can be used to identify content-specific language and vocabulary and plan for instructional supports.

Use this tool if . . . you are supporting students with developing content-specific vocabulary.

Revisit this tool . . . before new genre studies as you identify complex vocabulary and sentence structures.

To use this tool, you will need . . . familiarity with students' home language(s), genre-specific sentence structures, and vocabulary that matches students' development. Reading texts across this genre can help with determining this as well as referencing curriculum guides.

Make this tool your own by . . . trying the kind of writing that students will do, focusing on language that you use.

CHART 2.4

PLANNING STRUCTURES AND SUPPORTS FOR VOCABULARY DEVELOPMENT

Genre or Skill of Study: *Procedural writing unit*

CONTENT-SPECIFIC LANGUAGE STRUCTURES AND VOCABULARY	POSSIBLE INSTRUCTIONAL SUPPORTS
Sequencing and transition words (e.g., *first, second, after that*)	Vocabulary list supported by numerals
Prepositions of place (e.g., *above, below, in, next to, under*)	Genre-specific word wall with visual support
	Illustration with vocabulary labels
Direction-giving	Turn-taking with a partner to give directions and act out steps
	Sentence frames
Tip, warning	Nonwriting-related example
	Example in mentor text
	Labeled example in demonstration text

online resources ⇲ Available for download at **resources.corwin.com/responsivewritingteacher.**

In Chapter 1, we shared charts that help identify and prioritize skills for students who are multilingual. Chart 2.5 helps you to enumerate specific strategies and structures for working with students within various stages of English language acquisition.

Use this tool if or when . . . you have students in your classroom who are learning English at different stages.

Revisit this tool . . . as students develop English. The prompts can serve as a progression for both you and them.

To use this tool, you will need . . . to pay attention to what students understand and then say.

Make this tool your own by . . . adding prompts that work for you, keeping in mind the important balance of productive struggle and needed scaffolds.

CHART 2.5

PLANNING TO SUPPORT STUDENTS WITH EMERGING MULTILINGUALISM

12/1/2019 Example

STUDENTS	STAGE	PROMPTS	RESOURCES AND STRATEGIES
	Preproduction	Show me . . . Circle the . . . Where is . . . ? Who has . . . ?	Labels Pattern books Personal illustrated dictionaries
	Early production	Yes/no questions Either/or questions One- or two-word answers Lists Labels	Corrections for grammar and spelling after composition Wordless picture books that can be used to create stories
Rashan	Speech emergence	Why . . . ? How . . . ? Explain . . . Phrase or short-sentence answers	Grammatical structure Sentence frames with transition words
Amar TJ	Intermediate fluency	What would happen if . . . ? Why do you think that . . . ?	Lists of transitional words Opportunities for verbal practice
Seth Manu Kierra Sanara	Advanced fluency	Decide if . . . Retell . . .	Self-editing checklists Note-taking templates Lists of transitional words

Supporting Students With Expressive and Receptive Language Development

In Chapter 1, we provided tools for gathering information about students who are developing expressive or receptive language. Chart 2.6 can help build a repertoire of strategies to support receptive language, while Chart 2.7 can help develop instructional skills for supporting expressive language. The modifications listed may be made with specific students in mind but make learning more accessible for everyone.

CHART 2.6

PLANNING TO SUPPORT STUDENTS WITH EXPRESSIVE LANGUAGE DEVELOPMENT

IF A STUDENT IS CHALLENGED BY . . .	THEN . . .
Responding to questions	• Provide visual supports for questions. • Ask student questions ahead of time. • Cue that there will be a question coming up. • Provide extra wait time.
Telling stories	• Create story markers to use as scaffolds, such as *first, then, next, finally* for primary students or *a little later, meanwhile, after a while, just then, in the end* for upper-elementary students. • Model storytelling, and provide practice opportunities. Repeated storytelling can be really helpful for students!

Expressing feelings	• Create and provide talking prompts, such as the following:
	  • I'm feeling that . . .
	  • It surprises me that . . .
	  • I felt _____ when . . .

Participating and extending conversations	• Create and provide talking prompts, such as the following:
	  • This makes me think . . .
	  • Adding on to . . .
	  • In response to . . .

Using correct syntax	• Offer plenty of opportunities for verbal practice. • Focus on corrections that interfere with meaning while modeling correct usage.
Using and developing vocabulary	• Create vocabulary walls. • Expand vocabulary knowledge by teaching antonyms and synonyms. • Challenge students to use new words in speaking and writing.

online resources ⬀ Available for download at **resources.corwin.com/responsivewritingteacher.**

CHART 2.7

PLANNING TO SUPPORT STUDENTS WITH RECEPTIVE LANGUAGE DEVELOPMENT

IF A STUDENT IS CHALLENGED BY . . .	THEN CONSIDER . . .
Following directions	Cueing students that a direction is coming Using a visual to support the receptive language Adding nonverbal cues Creating predictable systems, structures, and routines for directions
Understanding questions	Limiting the complexity of questions Providing written copies whenever possible Teaching students to self-monitor and ask for clarification whenever necessary
Understanding stories and/or read alouds	Providing written versions whenever possible Giving students a summary or components to listen for ahead of time
Understanding and developing vocabulary	Preteaching vocabulary words Teaching students to use context whenever possible Supporting students to self-monitor and ask questions as well as use tools that are available for them

online resources 🔺 Available for download at **resources.corwin.com/responsivewritingteacher.**

CULTURALLY RESPONSIVE PLANNING

"Basic to a liberal arts education is the understanding that there is more than one way to see the world," wrote Emily Style, founding codirector of the National SEED Project, in a 1988 essay. A balanced curriculum, according to Style, is one in which students are engaged in disciplines of looking at the world through various "window" frames. Style (1988) continued, "The delightful truth is that sometimes when we hear another out, glancing through the window of their humanity, we can see our own image reflected in the glass of their window. The window becomes a mirror! And it is the shared humanity of our conversation that most impresses us even as we attend to our different frames of reference" (p. 1). In this balanced curriculum, which Style described as ideal for everyone, students gain the following:

Cultural Responsiveness ↓
Plan instruction that has . . .
Connections, content, and contexts that are reflective of diverse communities

- Knowledge of both self and others
- Clarification of the known and illumination of the unknown

Style (1988) also addressed the reality that curriculum, which was historically designed for white males, is not balanced if students see themselves in the mirror all the time: "Democracy's school curriculum is unbalanced if a Black student sits in school, year after year, forced to look through the window upon the (validated) experiences of white others while seldom, if ever, having the central mirror held up to the particularities of her or his own experience. Such racial imbalance is harmful as well to white students whose seeing of humanity's different realities is also profoundly obscured" (p. 5). A critical examination of curriculum leads to culturally responsive plans, which provide a balance of windows and mirrors for students not only in the classroom but in their communities and in the world.

Planning Connections, Content, and Contexts That Are Reflective of Diverse Communities

Culturally relevant teachers utilize students' culture as a vehicle for learning. —Gloria Ladson-Billings (1995)

With thoughtful planning, mirrors and windows can be woven into connections, tools, and share sessions. Referencing information gathered about student identities (using tools referenced in Chapter 1) is essential for planning instruction and resources. When deciding who to provide mirrors for and who to provide windows for, consider which subgroups (for example, race, language and dialect, family structure, gender, religion, ability, class, and nationality) have been marginalized, silenced, oppressed, and/or portrayed in problematic ways in mainstream media and literature. In classes composed of predominantly privileged groups, for example, this looks like prioritizing windows in curriculum, as mirrors are inherently present in much of their academic experience. Continuously, these students will still have certain aspects within these windows that mirror their own experiences. Powerful texts provide both windows *and* mirrors for children.

Throughout lessons, there are some predictable experiences and resources to keep in mind. For example, teachers build relationships with students by sharing stories and authentic purposes for lessons and work; these are connections and tools, such as charts (see Chapter 3), mentor texts (see Chapter 4), and demonstration texts (see Chapter 5) that all provide opportunities for students to see themselves and others in their world of learning. Additionally, teachers can amplify student work and voices during share sessions.

Some opportunities for mirrors and windows in your lessons include the following:

- *Connections*: Use of storytelling, photographs, and videos. Authentic purposes can also be made in introductions, including ones that connect with topics of social justice.
- *Tools:* Inclusive family structures, neighborhoods, cultures, and home languages can be represented In the illustrations, text, and content of tools such as charts, mentor texts, and demonstration texts.
- *Share sessions:* Student work, work by authors or illustrators, and photos and videos of authors or illustrators.

Chart 2.8 can be used to plan for aspects of instruction that will offer mirrors and windows for students. Figure 2.2 demonstrates how one teacher used this chart to plan how to weave identity throughout a persuasive writing unit.

Use this tool when . . . you are making intentional choices about who is represented in instruction.

Revisit this tool . . . when focusing on increasing engagement through more relevant contexts and connections.

To use this tool, you will need . . . to reference information about students (collected in Chapter 1) as well as become more familiar with aspects of the identities, relevant topics, and interests of students in and beyond the classroom representation to ensure authenticity.

Make this tool your own by . . . ensuring that your classroom's environment, resources, and strategies are not only inclusive of the students who are learning there but also inclusive of the world into which they are heading.

CHART 2.8
PLANNING FOR CULTURAL REPRESENTATION

Writing Unit: Information, Second Grade

Date: February 2020

ASPECTS OF IDENTITIES TO REPRESENT AS MIRRORS OR WINDOWS	POSSIBLE WAYS TO INCLUDE WITHIN CONNECTIONS FOR LESSONS IN THE UNIT *(i.e., videos and photographs to share, stories to tell, purposes for matters of social justice)*	POSSIBLE WAYS TO INCLUDE WITHIN TOOLS USED IN UNIT *(i.e., who/where/what is featured in the illustrations and content of classroom tools and resources)*	POSSIBLE WAYS TO INCLUDE WITHIN SHARE SESSIONS IN UNIT *(i.e., stories to tell, videos/ photos/work of authors and illustrators to highlight, connections to matters of social justice)*
Family traditions Black, Indigenous, and peoples of color (BIPOC) Nonbinary gender Athletes, female athlete-activists	In a connection, one purpose of writing is to teach the world about yourself and things you are an expert on. You might teach all about your family traditions or holidays, activities you do outside of school, places you like to go to, or topics you are passionate about.	Idea-generation tools—make a chart using pictures or drawings shared by families and of student interests or areas of expertise Demonstration texts: Write all about soccer (shared class interest), include chapters on the Women's Soccer Team and their work with equal pay and nonbinary gender inclusivity Mentor text: *Fry Bread: A Native American Family Story* by Kevin Noble Mallard (2019)	Highlight student work in share sessions that represents these aspects of identities. Watch the video of Kaitlyn Saunders performing over the Black Lives Matter mural. Show her Instagram page (@the.skate.kid), which teaches about skating and also inspires children to speak up/create/write about what they know or believe as a means of activism.

online resources ⤓ Available for download at **resources.corwin.com/responsivewritingteacher.**

Figure 2.2 A fourth-grade teacher made their own version of Chart 2.8 for a persuasive writing unit.

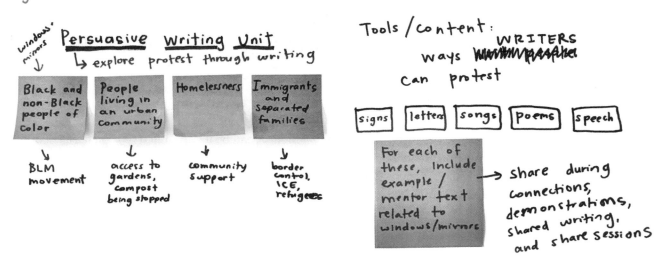

SOCIALLY-EMOTIONALLY RESPONSIVE PLANNING

Social-Emotional Responsiveness
↓
Plan instruction that has . . .
Writing experiences that are meaningful and align with student interests
Safe and supportive opportunities for students to take risks and work collaboratively

In *Engaging Children*, Ellin Oliver Keene (2018) proposes that there are four contributing factors, or pillars, of true engagement, as shown in Figure 2.3: intellectual urgency, emotional resonance, perspective bending, and the aesthetic world.

Keene references the *flow state*, a sensation of engagement, described in this way:

> There's this focus that, once it becomes intense, leads to a sense of ecstasy, a sense of clarity: you know exactly what you want to do from one moment to the other; you get immediate feedback. You know that what you need to do is possible to do, even though difficult, and sense of time disappears, you forget yourself, you feel part of something larger. And once the conditions are present, what you are doing becomes worth doing for its own sake. (Csikszentmihalyi, 1990, as cited in Keene, 2018)

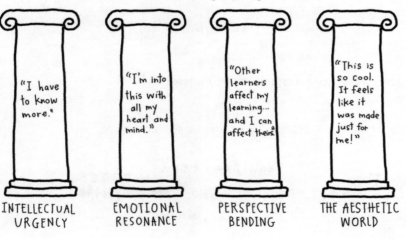

Figure 2.3

Perhaps you can think of a time you've been in a flow state, or have seen children enthralled in a read aloud or in their writing—not wanting to stop. One purpose of social-emotional responsiveness, when planning, is engaging students in this way. To do so, align content with student interests and invite students to take risks and collaborate in a safe environment.

Planning Meaningful Experiences That Align With Student Interest

Student interests and shared experiences can be incorporated into each aspect of instruction, including the illustrated connections and contexts, the tools that are used, and share sessions. Some ways to incorporate authentic experiences or student interests include the following:

- *Connections:* Analogies made to favorite places, things, and topics; telling stories of things or people students are interested in; connecting to shared experiences or purposes
- *Tools:* Within language(s), illustrations, content, and themes of classroom tools such as charts, mentor texts, demonstration texts
- *Share sessions:* Within stories told, videos and photos shared of students or people and characters they love

Chart 2.9 offers space to note interests and shared experiences (collected in Chapter 1) alongside space to brainstorm inclusion in instruction.

Use this tool as . . . you develop a history of experiences with your class. What stories have you all lived through together? What stories and experiences have students shared?

Revisit this tool . . . as the school year progresses and the list of shared understandings grows.

To use this tool, you will need . . . to reference information about student interests (see Chapter 1). It's also helpful to take pictures or videos or have a journal nearby to document moments of interest and shared experiences.

Make this tool your own by . . . reflecting, honoring, and highlighting the voices, experiences, and shared understandings of the students in your classroom.

CHART 2.9
PLANNING FOR MEANINGFUL EXPERIENCES AND SHARED INTERESTS

Chart 2.12 Meaningful Experiences and Shared Interests
Writing unit: Poetry
Date: March - April

Shared experiences: → big feelings → snow storm, N moving away, going to the park, plant dying, new class pet, seeing the hawk, baking	
Shared interests *(list by whole class or small group):* pizza! sharks, tree houses, baking, collecting things, pets, legos	
Individual interests: K-trains, roses B,H,G-birds E-Marvel B-bears, dolphins	

	Ways to incorporate authentic experiences or student interests
Connections	→ poets can get ideas from times they have big feelings, like the time we... or when we all ...
Tools	within examples on tools - imagery, metaphors, similes - incorporate interests "as sharp as a shark's tooth" → Read the Word Collector by Peter H Reynolds + connect to student collections + descriptive words
Share sessions	Write shared/interactive poems about shared experiences + interests

online resources Available for download at **resources.corwin.com/responsivewritingteacher.**

Planning Safe and Supportive Opportunities for Students to Take Risks and Work Collaboratively

Chapter 1 referenced ways that habits of mind relate to the writing process.

Chart 2.10 provides an example of a space to plan strategies and supports based on the traits of a growth mindset (Dweck, 2006).

Use this tool when . . . you are reinforcing the traits of a growth mindset with your classroom and you want to emphasize the opportunities for these thought processes within writing instruction.

Revisit this tool . . . if you are focusing on a particular trait.

To use this tool, you will need . . . to build familiarity with traits of a growth mindset with students—through class conversations and read alouds.

Make this tool your own by . . . highlighting particular mindsets and behaviors for the specific students in your classroom.

CHART 2.10
PLANNING TO SUPPORT BUILDING POSITIVE MINDSETS

STUDENTS	WRITING BEHAVIOR	STRATEGIES FOR SUPPORT
Dean Kyron Olivia	Perseverance	Self-talk prompts: • I know I can do this, but I'll have to work hard. • I won't give up. Teaching strategies: • Work plans • Goal cards
Manu Alex Kathleen	Empathy	Self-talk prompts: • How might my characters feel? • What would my audience need to know?
Kathleen TJ Sanique	Resilience	Self-talk prompts: • I can do this even though it's hard. • I won't give up. Revision tools: • Paper strips • Sticky notes • White cover-up tape

STUDENTS	WRITING BEHAVIOR	STRATEGIES FOR SUPPORT
Rashad TJ Sophia Alex	Flexibility	Self-talk prompts: • I will try this a different way. • Here's another approach . . . Resources for students: • Strategy charts (see Chapter 3) • Revision tools
Klerra Charlie Thomas	Optimism	Self-talk prompts: • I like my work because . . . • I am proud of the part where I . . . Charts that show the following: • Student progress • Current goals and achieved goals

online resources ☞ Available for download at **resources.corwin.com/responsivewritingteacher.**

Responsive Planning Across the Domains

While this book is structured so that each domain can be returned to when focusing on any given area of responsiveness, the domains are not mutually exclusive. The following classroom example shows how academic, linguistic, cultural, and social-emotional responsiveness become integrated in instruction.

Putting It in Practice

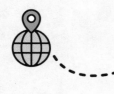

As a fifth grader, Jayda moved to Melanie's district in the winter. Jayda's teacher spent the first few weeks getting to know her and supporting the transition into a new community. He explored the neighborhood that Jayda moved from and enjoyed conversations with her friends and family. He noticed that Jayda lights up when she talks about the ocean and can outrun all of her peers outside. He discovered that Jayda is an artist, spending much of her choice times throughout the day drawing in a sketchbook that is always kept nearby.

During writing, Jayda was invited to freewrite in her first weeks of school. Her classmates were in awe of the way Jayda's attention to detail as an artist transferred to her voice as a storyteller. When it was time for her class to begin an information writing unit, it seemed that Jayda had not previously been immersed in the genre as a writer. Jayda's teacher was concerned that this would be a barrier to the research-based project that the class would engage in.

Jayda's teacher knew there were other students who were developing their sense of nonfiction writing. On a day when the class focused on research and note-taking, their teacher invited Jayda and a small group of students to write a few quick pieces about events in the past that they already knew about. On the following days, they learned how to plan sections, incorporate facts and their own thinking, and draft introductions and conclusions. Once Jayda learned the structure of information writing, she integrated all of the skills to incorporate a research component. Jayda's teacher did not lower expectations for what Jayda could do as a writer. He leaned on all that she had already developed as a writer to provide an alternate entry point for new work. By the end of the unit, Jayda met all of the benchmarks on the fifth-grade scope and sequence.

Digging Deeper

Throughout the chapter, we referenced specific resources. To read more about any of these concepts, we recommend the following books:

- *Every Child Can Write, Grades 2–5: Entry Points, Bridges, and Pathways for Striving Writers* by Melanie Meehan (2019)
- ¡Colorín Colorado! (https://www.colorincolorado.org), a bilingual website for educators and families of students learning English as a new language
- *Unlocking the Power of Classroom Talk: Teaching Kids to Talk With Clarity & Purpose* by Shana Frazin and Katy Wischow (2019)
- "Mirrors, Windows, and Sliding Glass Doors" by Rudine Sims Bishop (1990)
- *Culturally Responsive Teaching and the Brain: Promoting Authentic Engagement and Rigor Among Culturally and Linguistically Diverse Students* by Zaretta Hammond (2015)
- *A Teacher's Guide to Writing Conferences* by Carl Anderson (2018)

Tool for Planning Across the Domains

Planning

This tool can be used as a place to take notes, reflect, or expand upon the ideas in this chapter. Alternatively, it can also be used to plan for responsiveness across the domains.

Academic Responsiveness	Linguistic Responsiveness
• *Multiple entry points* • *Differentiated instruction*	• *Support for content-specific language and vocabulary as well as opportunities for students to write in multiple languages* • *Support for expressive and receptive language*
Cultural Responsiveness	**Social-Emotional Responsiveness**
• *Connections, content, and contexts that are reflective of diverse communities*	• *Meaningful work that is aligned with interests and shared experiences* • *Safe and supportive opportunities to take risks and collaborate*

online resources Available for download at **resources.corwin.com/responsivewritingteacher.**

CHAPTER 3

Co-Constructing Responsive Charts

Beyond the accessibility that charts bring to instruction, they are an asset to the classroom environment—blueprinting the work, ideas, and path toward shared goals. Susan Fraser and Carol Gestwicki (2012) write, "A classroom that is functioning successfully as a third teacher will be responsive to the children's interests, provide opportunities for children to make their thinking visible, and then foster further learning and engagement."

The class huddled around Katie Clements, Teachers College Reading and Writing Project (TCRWP) staff developer, who was visiting Kelsey's school, as she unveiled an envelope from her bag. Inside were photos of signs that Katie saw as she traveled throughout Japan. One by one, Katie enlarged the photos using a document camera, as children turned and talked, eager to collectively decode the meaning of the signs.

There were some aspects of each sign that seemed to have universal meaning, such as the one on the ice cream vending machine. Then, there were signs that required background knowledge that students were missing, such as the one that shows what is banned from an in-ground traditional Japanese toilet, *washiki toire*. Last, language was a barrier for most of the class, though several students who spoke Japanese proudly read the text aloud.

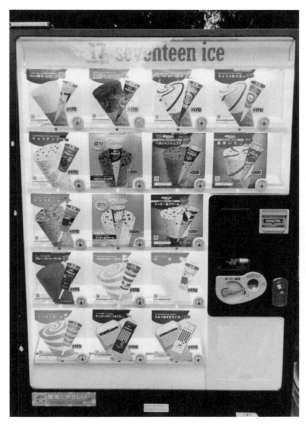

This experience expanded into an ongoing inquiry of signs and visuals in communities—in airports, on public transportation, in shopping centers, on social media, and even on commercials. Considering the purpose of the chart, then the language and images, we wonder the following:

- What is universal?
- Who is represented on this chart, and how? What implicit messages are sent as a result?
- How is language used to convey the message?

If these questions were to be asked about charts included in curriculum or found on internet sites, we imagine there may be universal qualities meant to reach a large population of students. But upon considering the text, upon looking critically at *who* is represented and *how*—the messages implicitly conveyed—we imagine curriculum charts can fall short. The responsive revisions made to precreated charts, or responsive decisions made when creating charts, not only affect how students will access charts but how students are impacted by charts—how children in our classrooms see (or don't see) themselves and others in the world.

Why Responsive Classroom Charts Matter

Classroom charts have the potential to be powerful resources for students. In fact, Universal Design for Learning (UDL) emphasizes the importance of representation, and charts provide visual representation when teaching a lesson and for independent practice. UDL also emphasizes access, and charts have to be readable, relatable, and understandable in order to impact learning.

When coaching in classrooms, one of Melanie's favorite questions to ask students is "What helps you learn?" Melanie then asks students to stand near something in the room that they use as support. If there are teacher-made charts, Melanie's action research results are that many students head to those first. "I understand them better since I was part of them being made," one student explained. Kelsey's action research around charts is based on observational data. She has found that students use charts most when they are placed at students' eye level, interactive, created with students, and/or mobile. Classroom charts also get more use when they show examples of students' work and photos of students as well as other high-interest content (see Figure 3.1).

Figure 3.1

Charts placed at students' eye level

Interactive charts

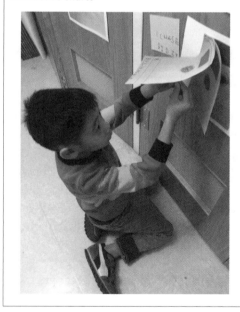

(*Continued*)

(Continued)

Charts made using photos of students or examples of student work	Charts created with students

Charts that are mobile	**Charts that include high-interest content**

Responsiveness with charts sometimes requires the modification of preexisting charts and sometimes requires the creation of new charts. Chart-making is a skill, and like many skills, the more you do it, the easier it becomes. Along the continuum of good to great classroom charts, it's possible to get to good pretty quickly. Knowing *how* to make charts for specific purposes and specific writers is empowering and an asset. We are not suggesting that every chart be original, however. We will show how existing charts can be modified so that they are more responsive to children in your classroom.

Melanie often reminded Kelsey, in writing this book, "Don't let perfect get in the way of good." Charts don't have to be perfect. Charts need to be *accessible* for students so they serve as a scaffold when students are practicing a skill and developing independence. Charts that are made with specific writers in mind may not be the most conventionally beautiful, but they are often the ones that are most used and most useful. Both teacher and students understand a responsive chart's purpose and meaning inherently. With this in mind, we continue to muster the courage to bring chart marker to paper, let go of perfection, and keep purpose at heart.

Tip for Tomorrow

1. Have a set of markers you love. We all write better with favorite pens!
    a. Kelsey's favorite chart-making tools include the following:
        i. Sharpie Pro Bullet Tip Permanent Markers
        ii. Crayola Art with Edge Thick & Thin Markers
        iii. Crayola Art with Edge Wedge Tip Markers
        iv. Crayola Multicultural Crayons

    e. Melanie's favorite chart-making tools include the following:
        i. Sharpie Pro Bullet Tip Permanent Markers
        ii. Sharpie Permanent Marker, Fine Point
        iii. Post-it Super Sticky Notes, 8 in. x 6 in., Rio de Janeiro Collection
2. Use sticky notes or removable labeling tape to make revisions.
3. Believe in the value of cross-outs. Doing so sends the message that mistakes are okay and a part of the writing process!
4. Just like books, charts can be made in drafts. A chart that has been made quickly alongside children can be remade during a prep or after school.
5. *Chartchums*, a blog created by Marjorie Antonelli and Kristine Mraz, is a wonderful resource for expanding your artistic repertoire. For quick mentor illustrations, search Boardmaker or enter "line drawing of _____" on Google Images.
6. Reflect students and their work. When you incorporate a photograph of a student doing the work described on the chart, you will increase the probability that students will look at—and then use—that chart. The same holds true for when you include students' work.
7. Add to charts over the course of a unit. That way you create a trail of your instruction and your students' learning that is visible and accessible.
8. Speaking of accessibility . . . make sure students can see charts, interact with them, and use them. You can create smaller versions or digitize them.
9. Remember: If students aren't using charts, then charts are playing the role of wallpaper—not learning tools.
10. When charts are outdated or no longer being used, "recycle" them by taking photographs of them and keeping copies in a binder for students to reference later on.

Types of Charts

Just as there are different tools to use for specific purposes, there are different charts to use for specific purposes. Each type of chart typically follows a consistent structure or contains similar elements based on the chart's purpose. With a purpose in mind, it's easier to decide upon which type of chart is needed, envision a structure, and model its use. As a guide for doing so, we've outlined the most frequent kinds of charts used in writing instruction (and in other content areas, as well). The following box details types of charts and their purposes, and Figure 3.2 shows photo examples of different types of charts from real classrooms.

Type of Chart	Purpose	Examples
Anchor chart	Describes elements of something	• Indicating characteristics of a genre • Detailing the jobs of writers during independent work time
Process chart	Guides students through the steps of a task	• Spelling a word • Writing a research-based essay
Strategy chart	Offers choices for developing a particular skill	• Adding a beginning • Bringing characters to life • Supporting a claim
Reference chart	Serves as a visual reminder of something used over and over	• Providing visual reminders of letters or words such as an alphabet chart or a word wall • Offering genre-specific vocabulary for quick access • Listing possibilities for generating ideas and topics
Checklist	Keeps track of one's completion of a task or process	• Revising and editing • Having independent writing routines
Goal-setting chart	Supports students with tracking progress toward a specific goal	• Finishing a certain number of books each week • Remembering to use punctuation • Elaborating with detail

Figure 3.2 Examples of Classroom Charts by Type

Type of Chart	Typical Layout	Example
Anchor chart	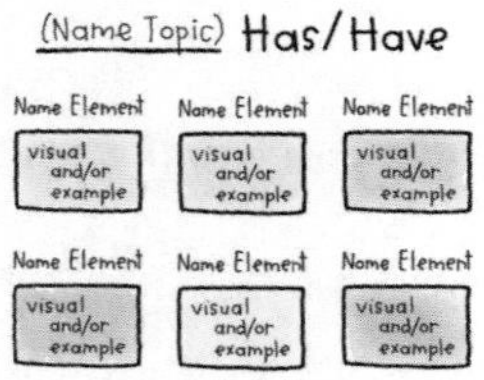	

Type of Chart	Typical Layout	Example
Process chart	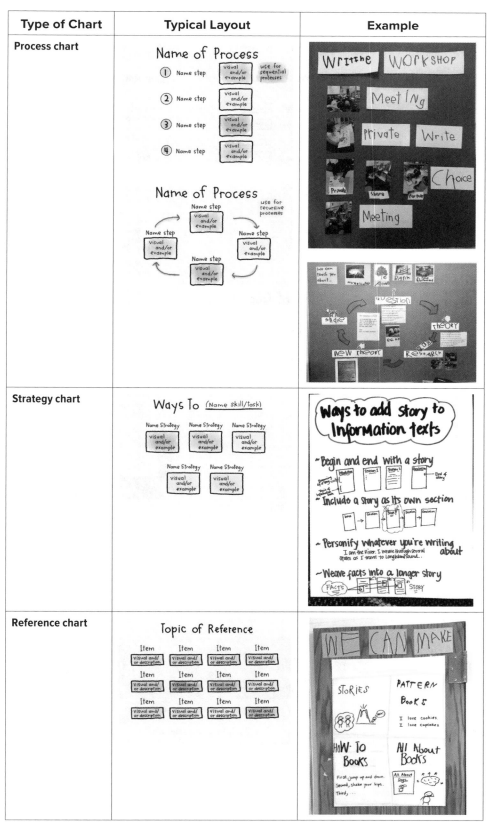	
Strategy chart		
Reference chart		

(Continued)

(Continued)

Type of Chart	Typical Layout	Example
Checklist	Name of Task ☐ Step or element [Visual and/or example] ☐ Step or element [Visual and/or example] ☐ Step or element [Visual and/or example] ☐ Step or element [Visual and/or example] *checkbox to track progress*	Opinion Writing Checklist ☐ I got my readers interested in my topic right at the beginning. (← hook your reader!) ☐ I stated my opinion. ☐ I used paragraphs to organize my reasons and ideas. ☐ I had reasons (at least 2!) that support my opinion. (One reason ___ is because ___) ☐ I explained and supported my reasons. Examples Facts Stories Statistics ☐ I used transitional words to connect my ideas. another for example Since also therefore ☐ I wrote a concluding statement or section.
Goal-setting chart	Name of Goal [visual and/or example] [visual and/or example] [visual and/or example] [INDICATOR] [INDICATOR] [INDICATOR] ☐ ☐ ☐ *checkbox to track progress*	

The first two chapters explored ways to assess and plan through the four domains of responsiveness. In this chapter, we share specific strategies to leverage charts for instruction and student independence in order to be responsive to and inclusive of students.

Academic Responsiveness ↓	**Linguistic Responsiveness** ↓	**Cultural Responsiveness** ↓	**Social-Emotional Responsiveness** ↓
Co-create charts that . . .			
Name a clear, relevant, and developmentally appropriate purpose Modify, extend, or supplement content	Use accessible, inclusive language(s), and provide definitions, examples, or visuals for new vocabulary Provide visual support for text	Reflect the cultural and social identities of students in text and visuals Incorporate student work in examples	Involve students in the creation process Incorporate the interests of students Offer support for relevant social-emotional skills and positive habits of mind

ACADEMICALLY RESPONSIVE CHARTS

Preparing for a weekly cleaning of the sensory table, kids each tried turning the nozzle to drain the water. "It's stuck!" they called, signaling for help.

"It would be so much easier if we had a *wrench*," Luna exclaimed.

Academic Responsiveness
Co-create charts that . . .
Name a clear, relevant, and developmentally appropriate purpose
Modify, extend, or supplement content

Luna's ability to name the tool she needed came from a clear purpose (a stuck nozzle) and an understanding of how tools work. Our hope is the writers in our classroom know which charts can support them with their work in this way. By *naming the purpose* of a chart and then *modeling its use*, we set children up for independence in *their* use and selection of classroom charts. This means we must also know the purpose and use of each chart prior to instruction.

When children are using charts, those charts are scaffolds, and therefore, students are aiming at approximation on the pathway toward mastery. The emphasis in writing classrooms should be on growth and learning. Sometimes this concept helps us create the most useful charts.

Determining a Clear, Relevant, and Developmentally Appropriate Purpose

To make academically responsive charts, consider the specific needs and goals of writers alongside unit plans (such as tools referenced in Chapters 1 and 2). The guiding questions that follow can help to frame thinking. For each question, consider skills (What will writers do?) and processes (How can they do it?).

When preparing for the beginning of a unit, ask the following questions:

- What will writers do?
- How can they do it?
- What strategies can help?

When preparing for the middle of a unit, ask the following questions:

- What are writers not doing yet?
- What might be getting in the way?
- What strategies might help?

When preparing for the end of a unit, ask the following questions:

- Where can writers go from here?
- What aspect of this work is particularly engaging for them or can be expanded upon?

Modify, Extend, or Supplement Content

We recommend determining the purpose first; then reference preexisting charts and consider the following:

1. Making modifications
2. Extending content
3. Creating supplemental charts

Making Modifications to Charts

Inspiration for charts often comes through observing students during independent writing time and focusing on where they get stuck. Notice what students do when they are stuck. Do they…

- Attempt any strategies?
- Shift focus to something else?
- Rely on you or peers for support?
- Utilize classroom resources?

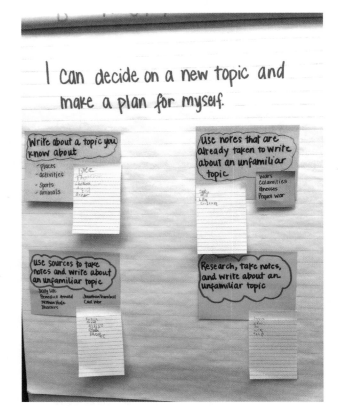

Figure 3.3 Fourth-grade students select their own starting points for a research-based informational writing unit.

From there, potential starting points and options emerge, suggesting ways to guide students toward independence.

Observations may show that some students need more explicit steps and instruction for skills or processes, such as idea generation, while other students might be ready for more elaborate methods in other areas, like revision. Modifications to charts provide responsive differentiation. Incorporating choices on charts also helps to offer multiple entry points for a skill or process, as shown in Figure 3.3.

It's important to consider how many choices students can be introduced to without becoming overwhelmed. Perhaps some students would do better by having one or two components added at a time, while others might benefit from exposure to more choices all at once. Sticky notes on charts offer flexibility in terms of how much information is on a chart to start. In the chart shown in Figure 3.4, the sticky notes offer examples of how each strategy could look, but those sticky notes don't have to be placed there until students are ready for them.

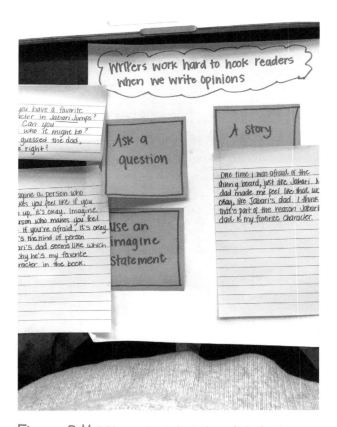

Figure 3.4 Fifth-grade students benefit by having strategy choices as well as examples as they work on their opinion essays.

Tip for Tomorrow

Ask students what strategies and processes (or charts!) work best for them. Many times, their input is the most accurate information we can obtain, and their self-assessment empowers them, builds self-efficacy, and increases engagement (Bandura, 1977; Hattie, 2012; McMillan & Hearn, 2008).

Extending the Content of Charts

Working through a grade-level curriculum unit, it's likely that charts are geared toward students who are functioning on or close to grade level. Yet there are likely students whose skills scatter across a wider spectrum.

Using the knowledge about Vygotsky's zone of proximal development (ZPD; refer to p. 52 in Chapter 2), overly difficult tasks run the risk of frustrating students, while overly simple tasks may disengage students. Creating a progression of charts will offer students choices about what they need support with and how they will grow. The chart in Figure 3.5 shows how this can be accomplished.

Figure 3.5 This progression was created to support kindergarten and first-grade students as they learn how to spell words with increasing complexity.

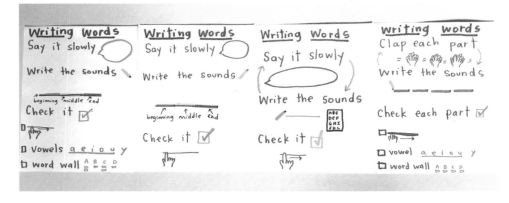

Additionally, anchor chart progressions are powerful and inviting tools for students. Try the following to make your own:

1. Read the standards for a specific genre or skill, beginning with the previous grade or grades. (Reference information-collecting tools from Chapter 1 to make sure the full range of student skills are supported.)

2. Create an anchor chart that describes what the text or skill looks like.

3. Continue this process, grade by grade, until you have a set of charts that shows the development of a skill for all students to access.

As another example, first- to third-grade standards for information writing were used to make the progression of anchor charts shown in Figure 3.6.

Figure 3.6 A progression of charts that increase in complexity offers students both support and challenge in an information unit.

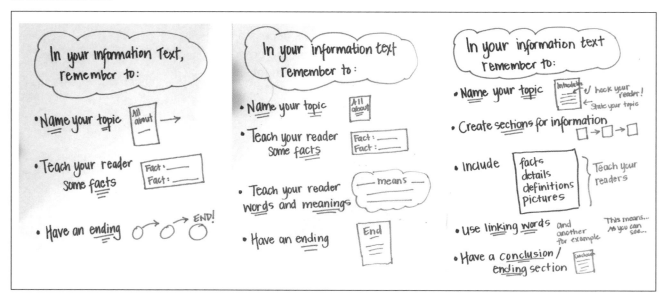

One way to present chart progressions to students is to ask them to choose the chart that feels *doable* to them but may be a little challenging. "Don't take/use the chart that feels overwhelming," you could say.

Remember to emphasize *growth* and not *mastery*. Students should feel comfortable choosing the tool that's right for them. You may be surprised at how responsibly and responsively students choose their own chart.

Creating Supplemental Charts

As more time is spent observing writers and determining specific challenges, it's likely you'll need charts that aren't yet in your repertoire. While we fully believe in staying connected on edu-communities, such as Twitter or Instagram, for inspiration in moments like this, it's important to feel empowered and equipped to make charts independently, as needed. Chart 3.1 makes it easier to explicitly name the steps to a process or skills for a strategy in order to make them more accessible to students. Figure 3.7 shows a teacher's sketched planning for a chart about characters' feelings.

Figure 3.7 A first-grade teacher sketched the layout and construction of a chart for showing characters' feelings during narrative writing.

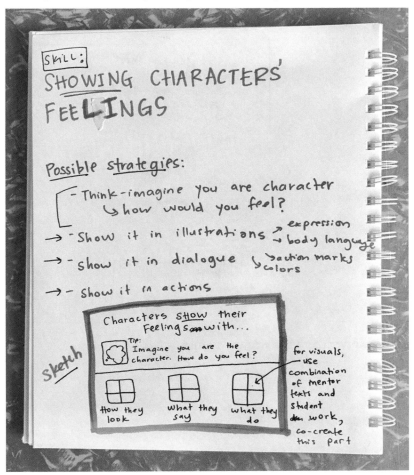

Use this tool when . . . you determine an area of challenge for students.

Revisit this tool . . . as new challenges arise throughout the year.

To use this tool, you will need . . . to spy on your own process as a writer. What is the cognitive work that you are having to do in order to be successful? Break that work down into the most concrete steps possible.

Make this tool your own by . . . considering and making transparent your own process. Understanding the work students are trying to do helps break it into steps that make sense to both adults and, in turn, students.

CHART 3.1

A CHART FOR PLANNING IN A FOURTH-GRADE NARRATIVE UNIT

Genre: Narrative

Skill or Process:

Planning how a story goes

Possible strategies:

- Beginning, middle, end
- Story mountain
- Timeline
- Pictures
- Sticky notes for scenes
- Slides presentation
- Anything else

Sketch layout of chart:

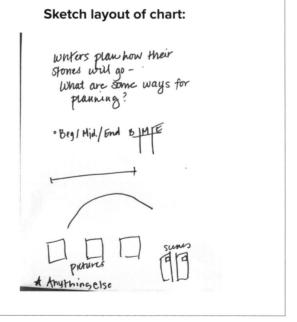

writers plan how their stories will go –
What are some ways for planning?

• Beg/Mid./End B/M/E

pictures

scenes

✱ Anything else

Tip for Tomorrow

Not everyone follows the same sequence of steps in order to be successful in a process, nor does everyone find the same strategies effective for developing a skill. Furthermore, great variety exists within and across genres. Such flexibility must also exist in tools—the kinds of tools, the content of them, and the choice of what and how to use them. Using language like "Ways to" or "_____ can have" or "Kinds of" in chart titles honors this variation in work.

Writing behaviors such as stamina and focus as well as utilizing classroom tools, working with a partner, and finding a just-right spot can also be supported with charts. Figure 3.8 shows a number of examples.

Figure 3.8

This chart shows options for partner writing after planning together: taking turns (seesaw) or writing together at the same time.

A classroom tracks students' stamina for independent writing on this graph.

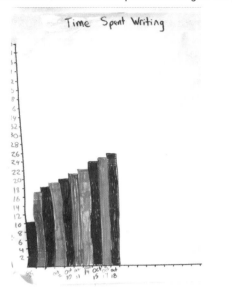

These charts were created with ideas from students, showing strategies for self-regulation, work spots, and productive writing talk.

LINGUISTICALLY RESPONSIVE CHARTS

Elijah stared at the easel from his writing spot, tears welling in his eyes. His class was working on a shared goal of finishing books each day. While brainstorming strategies, they came up with a saying, which was displayed on the easel: "Write and write, and never stop!"

Linguistic Responsiveness ↓
Co-create charts that . . .
Use accessible, inclusive language(s), and provide definitions, examples, or visuals for new vocabulary
Provide visual support for text

Elijah approached his teachers, clasping a book that he had not yet started, and said, "Do we really have to write and write *and NEVER stop?*"

Clearly, Elijah had taken this figurative language quite literally (something that is not uncommon for children to do). While Elijah's literal interpretation is common for young children, it is also common for students who are learning English, or students who have difficulty interpreting idiomatic language.

Elijah helped revise the chart for the class, who agreed: "Writers write and write until it is time to stop!" During share time, the class talked about how sometimes writers need to stop to take a little break, that taking a break sometimes helps writers write longer. They made another strategy chart, outlining different breaks writers can take (and limits for time spent taking a break).

The language that is used on charts is paramount for student understanding and use. Charts are linguistically responsive when text is accessible for all learners and inclusive of home language(s). Displaying charts helps to create a literacy-rich environment, which further nurtures language development (Goldenberg, 2008). Therefore, when children are using the language on the chart for specific and intentional purposes, the chart not only helps them build independence but also helps develop their language skills.

Visual supports also help build use and language, increasing linguistic responsiveness and making charts more accessible for students who are multilingual or who have speech and language-related impairments. *All* students benefit with more scaffolding to process and comprehend chart messages. Furthermore, though children typically fully develop language by the time they are eight, they can acquire content-specific vocabulary and language as well as figurative and expressive language at any age.

Making Language Accessible

The language of charts is more accessible when it matches students' reading and speaking abilities. The UDL principle of access comes into play when students can both *read the text* and *understand the text*.

When adding text to charts, one way to make it readable is to think about the reading levels of students. Think about the high-frequency words children can read and the typical structure and length of text they can decode. Figure 3.9 shows an example of three charts that use dots for children to point to while reading, high-frequency words, and visual supports to make them accessible.

Figure 3.9 This chart, which reminds kindergartners of what to do when they finish writing, also reinforces foundational print awareness.

Nazneen Patel, an upper-elementary teacher and instructional coach, adds the importance of students seeing their home language(s) on charts. She does this by including home language(s) that she has become familiar with, in phrases or expressions on charts, as well as in the text demonstrated on charts (e.g., in speech bubbles or through multilingual text). She also makes charts to support children, including children whose home language is African American Vernacular English (AAVE), translate to Academic English. She says, "It's important to write things as you say them. There are also times when you might read or write things in another way. Here's how that switch can look."

Language on charts can also be made more accessible when any content-specific vocabulary is supported by visuals, definitions, and/or examples. Visual representations are essential for supporting students with developing language and acquiring vocabulary (Fillmore & Snow, 2000). Though *all* children are still developing language and can benefit from this support, the visual components of charts support memory with multistep processes for children who are developing language-processing or receptive language skills. Figure 3.10 shows examples of how this might be accomplished.

Figure 3.10

This chart provides sentence starters to support elaboration within opinion writing. 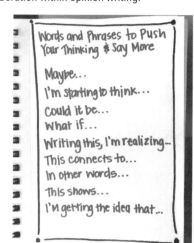	This chart shows students ways to develop vocabulary in writing. 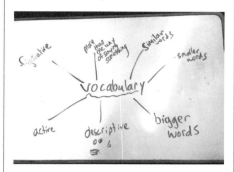
This chart supports students with sentence structures and transitional words for narrative writing. 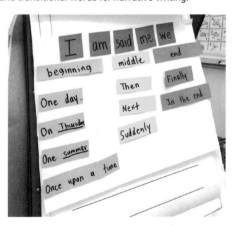	The sticky notes on this chart help students plan sentence structures and reinforce print awareness. 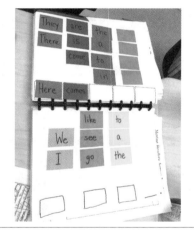

These tools were used by students, who were in a research-based informational writing unit, before including newly acquired vocabulary in their texts.

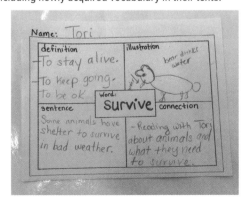

(Continued)

(*Continued*)

This chart describes ways to incorporate variety with language in narrative writing.

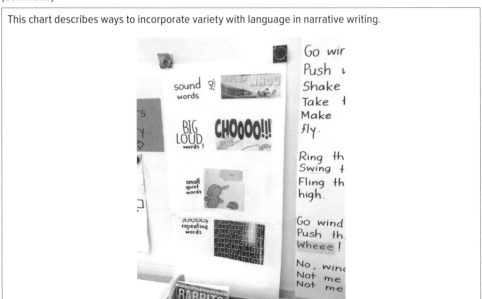

These charts provide visual support and sentence starters for giving feedback to each other.

CULTURALLY RESPONSIVE CHARTS

Cultural Responsiveness ↓
Co-create charts that . . .
Reflect the cultural and social identities of students in text and visuals
Incorporate student work in examples

Arlo spent days working on a chart for the door of his classroom: "WRITERS ARE HERE!" Arlo brought the idea to his teachers several days in a row in the week that they prepared for their first publishing celebration. Arlo shared his plan with the class, then recruited helpers during choice time. They stretched through each word carefully and presented it to their teacher, proud of the accomplishment.

"Wow! Now everyone will know that there are writers in this classroom. Wait a minute, how will people know *who* the writers are? What if people don't know *what* writers are? What could we do to make sure everyone who reads this knows *who* and *what* writers in this classroom are?"

"We can add a picture of writers!" several of the kids exclaimed.

"And what do writers look like?"

"They look like US!" Arlo squealed.

The chart makers then used the class name chart to add a picture of every member of their class, each holding a book or writing tool.

Any chart, like Arlo's, can be made with these questions in mind:

How can I show what this is?

How can I show what this looks like?

Then, most importantly, ask this question:

How can I show this in a way where students see themselves?

Charts that are culturally responsive reflect the identities of students in the content, in the visuals, and in the examples.

Reflecting the Cultural and Social Identities of Students

Our many identities make us who we are. They help others to understand who you are and help you to know more about the folx who are in your life and in the world. They connect us and they divide us. —Tiffany Jewell (2020)

An important element of culturally responsive teaching is that students see diverse representation within the classroom environment and its resources. What messages will students see about themselves and the world when they look around? Consider the major social identifiers of which people identify—race, language, family structure, gender, religion, ability, class, and nationality—and then consider if a classroom environment welcomes and includes those identities.

In looking at information collected about students' identities (see Chapter 1), think about which groups of students already see themselves represented in literature and the classroom environment. Who often requests to share and has a dominant voice? Which aspects of students' identities carry privilege and dominance in the world?

Then, prioritize bringing visibility and representation to students and aspects of their identity that have been historically marginalized. Deconstruct social norms about family structure, gender, and ability. Bring the kind of inclusiveness to charts that is needed in the literary world.

When creating visuals for charts, keep the aspects of student identities that will be represented in mind, while asking the following questions:

- *Who* is in this visual?
- *What* are they doing?
- *Where* are they?

Then, think about how to bring authentic representation through drawings and photographs. The examples in Figure 3.11 show a number of ways to do this using mentor texts, teacher-made drawings, co-constructed drawings, and photographs of students.

Figure 3.11 Bringing Authentic Representation to Charts

Using Mentor Texts:

Looking for Bongo, by Eric Velasquez (2016), is incorporated in this chart for narrative writing.

Illustrations and text elements from mentor text—*Yo! Yes?*, by Chris Raschka (2007)—are incorporated in this chart.

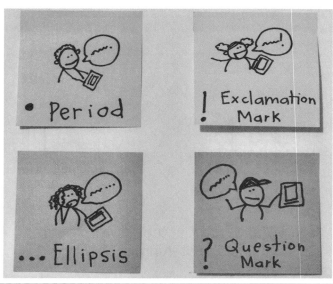

Using Teacher-Made Drawings:

The drawings on this chart show purposes of writing in the world.

Illustrations on this chart support students with sharing their thinking during class meetings and conversations.

The drawings on this chart offer choices for sitting during meetings.

(Continued)

Using Co-Constructed Drawings:

Students illustrate the drawings for the co-constructed ideas on this chart, which is kept near the meeting area and classroom agreements.

Student illustrations are incorporated on a chart to show how to add dialogue to books.

Using Photographs of Children:

Photographs of students throughout the school day are added to schedule cards.

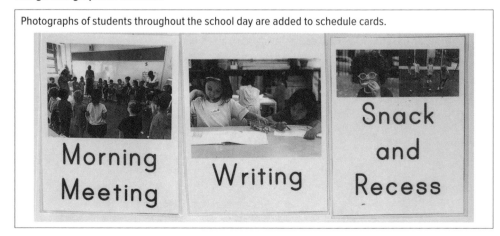

Photographs of students hang on this class name chart, which students can reference when writing stories about each other.

Student work is portrayed alongside mentors on this chart.

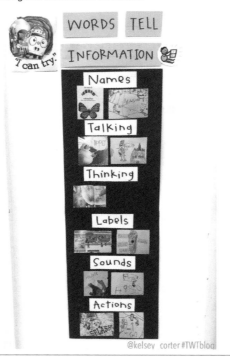

Tip for Tomorrow

Growing a habit of taking pictures and videos during independent writing time or even during lessons helps with having them available to include on charts. When school printers are not available, our colleagues have purchased classroom printers and ink by receiving donations from sites such as GoFundMe.

Many school districts have a disclaimer that caregivers sign in order to take and use pictures and videos of students for use on school websites and publications.

You can find one that can be modified or tweaked to use with students on the companion website at resources.corwin.com/responsivewritingteacher.

Incorporating Student Work in Examples

Another way to represent students inclusively is through the use of their ideas and writing in charts. Not only is doing so super engaging and empowering for children, but also it highlights students as authors who can teach and inspire.

When selecting student work, follow the same process of bringing representation to students who don't typically see themselves reflected as writers or in books. Some teachers we've worked with have found it helpful to keep a log to record whose ideas and work has been shared or replicated on charts. Figure 3.12 shows a couple of examples of charts that incorporate student ideas and student writing on classroom charts.

When including student ideas and work on charts, do the following:

- Co-construct a chart together during a minilesson or share session by recording student ideas, or students can add their own ideas to a chart using sticky notes.
- When a student shares an idea or thinking during a lesson or independent writing time, it can be shared with the class and quoted on charts.
- Look through writing folders for work that can be used as an example on a chart.

- To represent a specific student, preview a skill with them in a conference or small group, then photocopy their work for the chart.
- *Ask permission.* "I noticed you did (name skill) as a writer. I think it would help lots of kids in our class if they got to study your work. Would it be okay with you if I took a picture or made a copy of your writing to share with the class?"
- Name the writer while referencing their work on the chart: "Just like the author (student name) did here."
- Invite the student to join in on the teaching ahead of time: "Later today when I share your writing, would you like to show and talk about it together, or do you prefer to tell me about what you did and then I can share it with the class?"

Figure 3.12 Charts That Incorporate Student Work

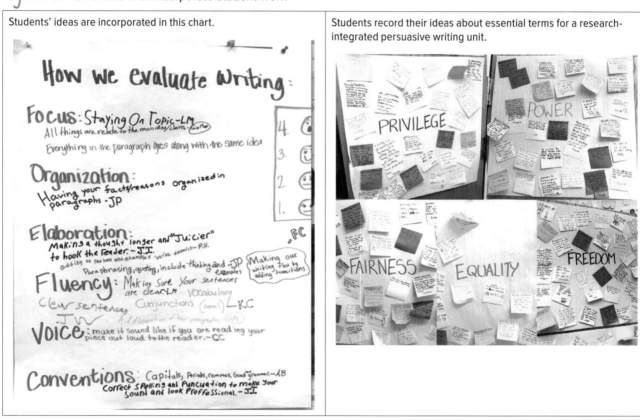

Students' ideas are incorporated in this chart.

Students record their ideas about essential terms for a research-integrated persuasive writing unit.

(Continued)

(Continued)

Students record ideas for purposeful writing, thinking about *why* they write and *who* they are writing for.

Elements of narrative writing are highlighted on student work within this chart.

Student work is added to the revision strategies on this chart.

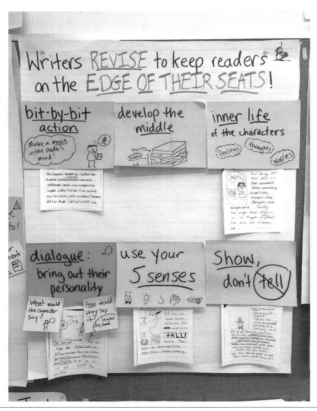

SOCIALLY-EMOTIONALLY RESPONSIVE CHARTS

Oliver was beaming throughout the day, thinking ahead about a playdate scheduled after school. "I have something very important to write today," Oliver said to his teacher at the beginning of independent writing time, "but it's not what we are working on right now. I need to remember all of the things I want to do on my playdate."

His teacher mirrored the serious look on Oliver's face. "That does sound very important. Do you have a picture in your mind for how you might do that?" Oliver nodded with confidence. "It sounds like you have been thinking about writing at other times of the day. That happens to me too—and lots of writers that I know! I think you should definitely get to work on this now. I can't wait to learn about your playdate."

Oliver's teacher went with him to the writing center, where they agreed that blank paper would be the best choice. He showed Oliver some different ways that he plans visually, then Oliver used a ruler to sketch boxes across the page, resulting in a sequential map for the playdate.

Oliver used his chart to teach his friend and caregiver before the playdate began. As they completed each activity on the agenda, Oliver added a check in the corner. Then, the chart found a new home on Oliver's bedroom wall, an artifact he could use before the next playdate.

Social-Emotional Responsiveness ↓
Co-create charts that . . .
Involve students in the creation process
Incorporate the interests of students
Offer support for relevant social-emotional skills and positive habits of mind

Involving Students in the Creation of Charts

When students participate in the creation of a chart, they not only feel more empowered to use it, but also they understand the concept on the chart better. Students can contribute to both writing and drawing on charts—remember, charts don't have to be perfect. (Chapter 6 provides additional examples of student-created charts.)

The following are ways students can be actively involved in chart creation:

1. Mirroring a shared writing session, students can help dictate ideas for content, text, images, or examples on a chart, while the teacher does the recording. This can take place during the minilesson or the share component of writing workshop.

2. Mirroring an interactive writing session, students can help record labels or drawings on the chart. This can take place during the minilesson or the share component of writing workshop. (Sketching lines with a light-colored marker is helpful to show students where the labels go. It's also a great time to show students that crossing out mistakes is okay!)

3. A small group of students (three or four) can help create the chart before it is shared with the whole class. This can be done during independent writing time, in any choice time throughout the day, or during a morning soft start. Students can be asked who would benefit from small-group interactive writing and drawing or who would benefit from previewing the content on the chart. Alternatively, ask for student volunteers who are interested in helping with the chart.

Incorporating the Interests of Students

When determining the content of a chart, include shared interests (or personal interests when the chart is for an individual student) wherever possible. This engages students when referencing the chart during instruction and brings them back to reference the chart as they need it. Interests can be included in a number of ways:

- In the language of a chart, incorporating lines from favorite songs, movies, or books
- In the drawings or photographs
- In the theme of the chart

Figure 3.13 shows classroom examples of each of these.

Figure 3.13 Classroom Charts That Incorporate Students' Interests

| Lyrics from Taylor Swift's "Invisible String" are incorporated on a chart for figurative language. | Students took photographs in small groups of items in the classroom and community environment to include on an alphabet chart. |

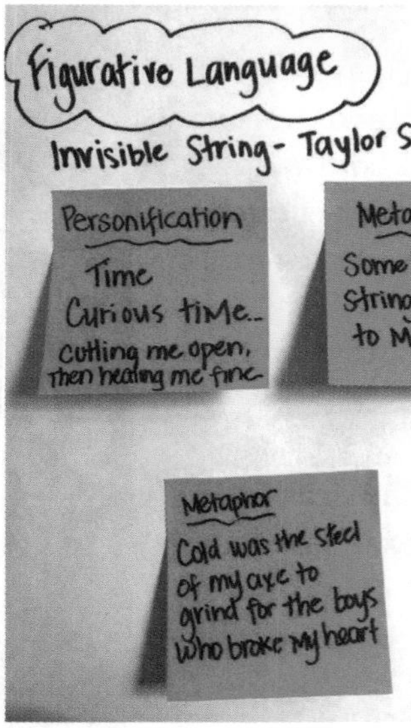

These charts (adapted from TCRWP Kindergarten Units of Study), used for reading and writing foundational skills, incorporate Ninjago.

Offering Support for Social-Emotional Skills and Positive Habits of Mind

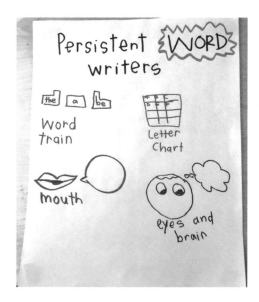

Charts can support social-emotional skills in various ways; they can reinforce a growth mindset with positive self-talk, provide flexibility for challenging skills, develop writing behaviors, and offer strategies for partner and conversational work.

The following table shows how traits of a growth mindset can relate to writing.

Trait	Relation to Writing
Resilience	Trying a new skill
Stamina	Remaining on task/working on a piece throughout workshop
Flexibility	Trying new strategies, revising a piece
Optimism	Believing that a new skill is possible
Empathy	Considering audience or imagining how characters would react and relate
Self-direction	Getting started on writing projects, seeking tools when stuck

Charts can support students with positive habits of mind and social-emotional skills while they write. Figure 3.14 shows a number of examples of classroom charts that provide social-emotional support to young writers.

Figure 3.14 Charts that provide social-emotional support

This chart illustrates neurons that can grow in the brain as a growth mindset develops.	Students share times they are flexible on this chart, which also includes positive self-talk.
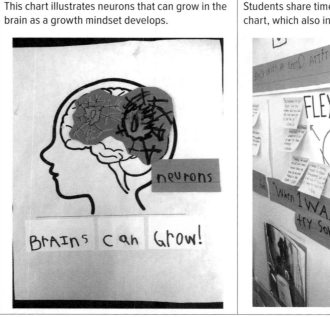	

This chart illustrates how traits of a growth mindset (with visuals for empathy, resilience, persistence, and optimism) can lead to ideas for stories.

A teacher brainstorms self-talk prompts for an informational genre study.

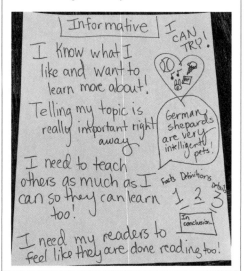

A Mood Meter, developed by the Yale Center for Emotional Intelligence's RULER, helps students with developing self-awareness.

This break spot offers strategies for self-regulation.

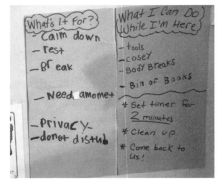

(Continued)

(*Continued*)

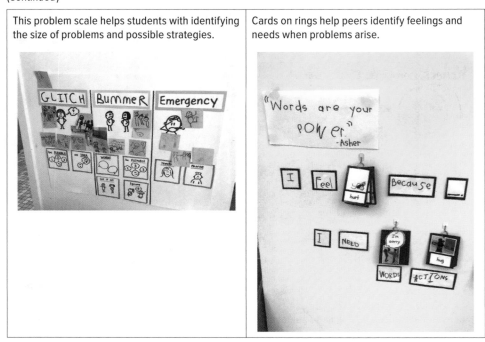

| This problem scale helps students with identifying the size of problems and possible strategies. | Cards on rings help peers identify feelings and needs when problems arise. |

Responsive Charts Across the Domains

While this book is structured so that each domain can be returned to when focusing on any given area of responsiveness, the domains are not mutually exclusive. The following classroom example shows how academic, linguistic, cultural, and social-emotional responsiveness can become integrated in instruction.

Putting It in Practice

All throughout the day, a group of children huddled around these bulletin boards—some, using a photo to storytell with a friend; some, making connections to the photos of their peers; some, writing alongside it, studying the details in photos to incorporate in their illustrations. Day after day, week after week, this became the most-frequented chart in the classroom.

Inspiration for the chart came after a number of students had trouble generating ideas during a personal narrative writing unit. Some writers sat, staring at blank paper for much of independent writing time. Others relied on adult support, saying, "I don't know what to write about."

Their teacher wanted to support writers with idea generation but also knew it was important to equip children with strategies and self-talk for when they don't know what to write about. As a writer, their teacher had experienced writer's block, and overcoming this challenge would be a skill students could rely on for the rest of their lives.

So, before each new genre study, the class shared ideas through class conversations, photographs, and drawings—simultaneously growing stronger as a community:

- What could you teach someone how to do?
- What topics do you know a lot about?
- What is a time you felt sad/scared/excited/proud?
- What do you like to do outside of school?
- What problems do you notice in our school? In the community? In the world?

Not only did the children have high-interest topics incorporated into the skill of idea generation, but also they were supported by strategies for independent problem-solving.

Digging Deeper

Throughout the chapter, we referenced specific resources. To read more about any of these concepts, we recommend the following books:

- *Smarter Charts K–2: Optimizing an Instructional Staple to Create Independent Readers and Writers* by Marjorie Martinelli and Kristine Mraz (2012)

- *DIY Literacy: Teaching Tools for Differentiation, Rigor, and Independence* by Kate Roberts and Maggie Beattie Roberts (2016)

- *Writing Strategies* by Jennifer Serravallo (2017)

- "Personal Goal-Setting: Planning to Live Your Life Your Way" by Mind Tools Content Team (n.d.)

- *Permission to Feel* by Marc Brackett (2019)

Tool for Planning Across the Domains

Co-Creating Charts

This tool can be used as a place to take notes, reflect, or expand upon the ideas in this chapter. Alternatively, it can also be used to plan for responsiveness across the domains.

Academic Responsiveness	Linguistic Responsiveness
• *Name a clear, relevant, and developmentally appropriate purpose.* • *Modify, extend, or supplement content.*	• *Use accessible, inclusive language(s), and provide support for new vocabulary.* • *Provide visuals for texts.*
Cultural Responsiveness	**Social-Emotional Responsiveness**
• *Reflect cultural and social identities in text and visuals.* • *Incorporate student work.*	• *Co-create with students.* • *Incorporate interests.* • *Support social-emotional skills and positive habits of mind.*

CHAPTER 4

Selecting Responsive Mentor Texts

Mentor texts provide students with inspiration and examples of writing elements specific to each genre. Making thoughtful choices about the texts for each unique class of writers is paramount, considering the content, language, and representation within the text and in the authorship. Such decisions can increase the connection children make with texts and authors; the connection children make with each genre; and the connection children make with themselves, as growing writers.

"How long did it take to make those books?"

"When did you start writing and at what age?"

"Which book is your favorite book out of every book you wrote?"

"What is your next book going to be about?"

Children and their families came to school on a Saturday, questions in tow, for an author visit with Zetta Elliott, a Black feminist poet and author. The school community had just finished reading *The Dragon Thief* (Elliott, 2019) for a book club. The most anticipated question was this:

Why do you write books about dragons? Why do you create a fantasy world?

Zetta answered:

> When I was little, I read books about magical creatures. I write about magic because I'm still into it. But I also write about magic because when I was a kid and I was reading magical stories, there was never anybody who looked like me in those stories. So I sort of had to dream myself into existence . . . . Magic is for everyone.

Zetta went on to explain that the first book she wrote for children, as a high schooler, was a magical story with all white characters and a family that did not look like hers. She wrote, in an article, "I had been invisible for so long that I automatically erased myself without ever considering that I had a *right* to create and inhabit magical worlds."

Zetta describes her childhood imagination as colonized—and is far from alone in her experience. Many other author-activists, like Jason Reynolds, Grace Lin, and Matt de la Peña, have also spoken about writing books for young people that they didn't have growing up. As more inclusive options are growing in literacy works, mentors can be found to not only inspire great writing but to inspire a pursuit of authorship as well.

Why Selecting Mentor Texts Matters

Many definitions of *mentor* include the word *trust.* In fact, Stacey Shubitz (2016) writes in *Craft Moves,* "Authors are like trusted colleagues we invite to teach alongside us. Their books inspire us, their personal stories and struggles resonate with us, and they show us new ways of understanding. We welcome authors we trust into our classrooms to help us teach our students strategies that will help them become better writers" (p. 15).

Trust, which is inherently personal—a dynamic within one's self and between people— is ever present in the heart work of responsive teaching. It calls for critical questioning:

- Who are the teachers students need to see?
- Whose stories do students need to hear?
- What ways of knowing/making do students need to learn?

The texts deemed trustworthy of close study must reinforce the trust within children that they, too, *make*—and *belong in*—the books of their imagination.

Trusted people and places that Melanie returns to when searching for classroom texts are not the same as Kelsey's. So, while many people seek recommendations as replacements for authors or books that are outdated, problematic, or nonrepresentative of diverse communities, we hesitate to provide lists of books without knowing the children who will be holding them.

Over the years, we have curated our own (ever-evolving) collections of books and authors that we consider mentors—ones that match developmental text features, ones with text that children love to recite and return to, ones that center underrepresented identities. Our bookshelves grew from conversations with colleagues (it's no secret teachers like to talk about books), particular topics of relevance for our classrooms, recommendations in blogs and at conferences, and from digital search engines. We share some of these resources in this chapter, as well as processes that have helped us select books that speak to young writers.

More than anything, our book collections grow from hours of perusing—Kelsey, nestled among stacks of books on the floor of her local bookstore, and Melanie, frequenting her favorite aisles of the school and neighborhood library. From these searches have come the most treasured mentor texts—and an understanding of how unbalanced representation is in published literature. There is a movement happening to change this representation, but until it mirrors the diversity of our population at large, we will continue to search for and hold the spotlight on books and authors that children need.

Types of Mentors

As writers and teachers of writing, we study and differentiate between *mentor authors* (and illustrators!) and *mentor texts,* and we refer to both in classrooms. Mentor authors are people who write books, and we may study a specific text they have authored and their body of work, as well as their explanations of their process and the similarities and differences between their various texts. On the other hand, when we say mentor text, we are referring to the text itself, written by an author/illustrator. We use that text to identify, highlight, and inspire specific craft moves and strategies within a genre, unit, or lesson. *Note: When a text is selected, we reference both the author as a mentor and the text itself.* Figure 4.1 demonstrates the differences between these two terms and how they might appear in our instruction.

Figure 4. 1 Mentor author or mentor text?

	Mentor Author/Illustrator	**Mentor Text**
What is it?	The person who creates the text or A body of work by the same author/illustrator	A single text written by an author/illustrator
When might it be used?	During a genre study, if the author's work represents a consistent genre During a non–genre-specific study, such as an illustration study, an independent writing project unit, or a study that focuses on writing processes/behaviors	Throughout a genre study or as part of a specific lesson
What might be the focus?	• Author visits or recorded interviews—finding topics, writing process, challenges, and inspiration • Compare and contrast text features or craft moves • Voice • Illustrations • Variety in genre	• Engaging beginnings or introductions • Establishment of setting • Use of figurative language and/or description • Variation of sentence length and/or grammatical structures

Responsive Mentor Texts Across the Domains

Throughout this chapter, we explore questions and tools for mentor text selection and use, considering academic, linguistic, cultural, and social-emotional responsiveness. Like many of the chapters in this book, it's suggested to revisit the ideas and tools once information about students is gathered and throughout the school year (see Chapter 1). It is also helpful to work alongside plans (see Chapter 2).

Academic Responsiveness ↓	Linguistic Responsiveness ↓	Cultural Responsiveness ↓	Social-Emotional Responsiveness ↓
Select mentor texts that . . .			
Are accessible to students as readers and writers Match text elements and craft moves that students can approximate	Provide support for processing, especially in multilingual texts Contain support for language, such as labels, repetition, illustrations, definitions, or captions	Include mirrors and windows for students within the authorship, content, text, and illustrations Prioritize representation for those who have been historically underrepresented within the literacy world	Match relevant topics and/or interests of students with topics and story lines in the mentor texts Incorporate social-emotional support and/or positive habits of mind

SELECTING MENTOR TEXTS FOR ACADEMIC RESPONSIVENESS

Academic Responsiveness ↓
Select mentor texts that . . .
Are accessible to students as readers and writers
Match text elements and craft moves that students can approximate

When Melanie tries to improve her tennis game, her go-to mentor is Serena Williams. Melanie plays videos from Serena's matches, zeroing in on a specific stroke or strategy. Melanie doesn't expect to hit a forehand or serve an ace with the precision and power of Williams, but studying the process helps her become incrementally better. Doing so, Melanie is *approximating* skills of Serena Williams but is far from the level of mastery—in much the same way that young writers approximate work of authors in published texts. In fact, Melanie frequently shares this connection with students as they study published work.

When getting to know mentor authors and using mentor texts, it's important to emphasize that the expectation is not for students to write "just like a published author or text" but instead to find inspiration in the author's work. There is an important distinction between approximation and mastery, especially when considering mentor texts. It's our hope that every young writer takes risks and tries something new. It's unlikely anyone will be great at something the first (or second or third) time it's tried. In fact, if students are great too soon, then they might not be trying the right new task. (Remember the importance of the zone of proximal development [ZPD] from Chapter 2.) Approximation should be noticed and celebrated, as it leads to intentional practice and growth!

Tip for Tomorrow

Name moments when you, students, or characters approximate something. While you may not use the word *approximate,* you might say, "I've never tried this before," or "This is really hard for me," or "I'm going to watch how (name mentor) does it first," or "Did you notice how (name student or character) got better at _____ after watching someone else?" Doing so not only sends the message that other people can help us learn and grow, but it also reinforces a growth mindset.

Selecting Accessible Mentor Texts

When making academically responsive decisions about mentor texts, consider readability and writability. By readability, we mean the ability of students to comprehend the text as readers and the ability to reference back to the text, using both illustrations, print, and accessible language(s). By writability, we mean the ability of students to approximate the author's craft and genre-specific components in their own writing.

The most high-impact mentor texts should be both readable and writable for students because students need to be able to access the text in order to appreciate and emulate the craft moves within it. If a child is struggling with comprehending or decoding a text, frustration may deter that child from wanting to reread and apprentice themselves to any element or lesson that the text may offer.

Because students will first experience a mentor text as a reader, we recommend first looking at a mentor text through the lens of students as readers. When doing so, consider whether the length and content match current read alouds, shared reading texts, or independent reading levels (leveled texts can make great mentor texts in lower grades!).

Once a mentor text is selected, making it accessible first involves close and repeated reading. A possible introduction to a mentor text can evolve like this:

1. Read the mentor text at the typically scheduled read aloud time. Even if this is a book students have read before, reread it to build comprehension.

2. Plan places to stop and *think aloud* as the reader and places for students to stop and *turn and talk* with a partner. Again, the initial focus should be on comprehension.

3. Decide if students need to read the book again *to comprehend it* before looking closely at it *as writers*. A second reading during read aloud time can be helpful. The focus can be on noticing even more details as readers.

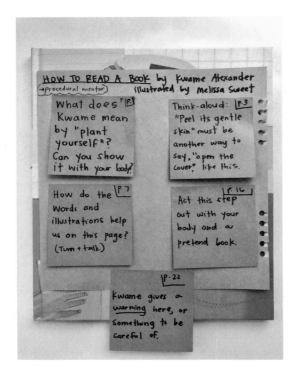

Prompts for processing during read aloud are added for the mentor text, *How to Read a Book,* by Kwame Alexander (2019).

4. During a subsequent read aloud time (as it may take longer than the recommended length of a minilesson), reread the book—this time, as writers. This can be done by using the mentor text chart (see Chart 4.1) and through a guided study or inquiry. In a guided study of a mentor text, students should pay attention to certain text features or craft moves. In an inquiry, students should be sharing what they notice, and teachers can help with the specific naming of elements or craft moves.

5. Annotate the text using sticky notes and/or highlighter tape, and then make a chart (such as Chart 4.1) to record craft moves and text elements. This will support students with referencing back to the text independently.

6. Make the text available to students (some teachers include a mentor text bin), or photocopy annotated pages to include in the writing center, student folders, or as an example on charts.

7. Continue to lean on the mentor text throughout the unit of study, referencing it as you teach into specific skills and strategies.

Matching Skills and Craft Moves That Students Can Approximate

One goal for a mentor text is for students to read a text and think *I can do that too* instead of *That writer is so good. . . . I could never be that good.* To make sure features in a mentor text can be approximated by students, read it alongside a genre-specific anchor chart, rubric, or trajectory, and consider the following:

1. Does the text model many of the genre-specific elements and craft moves that students will learn to include in their writing?

2. Will students be able to notice how and where the elements/craft moves are featured?

3. Will students be able to approximate such text features?

One tool that can be helpful for looking at a mentor text closely and planning for parts of the text to study is a mentor text chart, such as Chart 4.1, which can be used for several purposes. It can be used to make plans for a mentor text, then referenced when studying a mentor text with students. Additionally, it can be co-created with students. By projecting the chart on a document camera, or creating a larger version, students can stop and notice craft moves and text features as the teacher reads aloud. The teacher can name and record the noticings on the chart. And a copy of the co-created chart can be kept in the inside of the mentor text for students to reference on their own (see Figure 4.2).

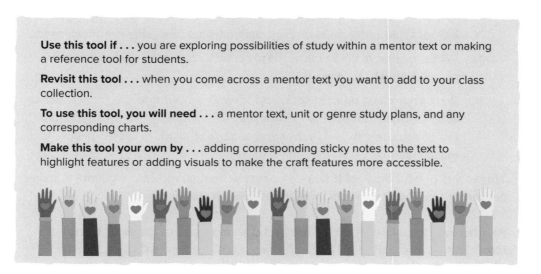

Use this tool if . . . you are exploring possibilities of study within a mentor text or making a reference tool for students.

Revisit this tool . . . when you come across a mentor text you want to add to your class collection.

To use this tool, you will need . . . a mentor text, unit or genre study plans, and any corresponding charts.

Make this tool your own by . . . adding corresponding sticky notes to the text to highlight features or adding visuals to make the craft features more accessible.

CHART 4.1
MENTOR TEXT CHART TEMPLATE

A Different Pond by Bao Phi (2017)

PAGE NUMBER	CRAFT MOVE
1–2	Establishment of characters and details
4	Use of similes
7–8	Blending of thoughts and talk
7–8	Establishment of setting
10	Establishment of setting through character action
12	Use of action to stretch important part
13	Blending of action and thought
16	Incorporation of backstory
18	Blending of action and description
20	Blending of action and inner thinking
21	Setting
25	Flash-forward
26	Final thought to end

online resources ⌕ Available for download at **resources.corwin.com/responsivewritingteacher.**

To make a mentor text chart, such as the one shown in Chart 4.1, follow these steps (individually, with colleagues, with a class, or with a small group of students):

1. Number the pages if the text does not already include page numbers. It doesn't matter where the numbering begins as long as it's consistent or students can follow the numeration.

2. Name the chart with the title of the text as well as the author's name and the illustrator, if there is one.

3. Include a column for page numbers, craft moves, and/or genre-specific elements.

4. While reading, make a note of the pages each craft move or element that you plan to highlight appears.

5. Copy your chart on cardstock, and leave it tucked into the front cover to access while studying the mentor text with students. An illustrated chart can be made and tucked in the cover to allow students to use the mentor text independently.

This tool is helpful because it helps to create accessible tools for students to independently access craft moves in mentor texts of their choice.

Another way to make the text features and craft moves more accessible to students is to create choices that offer a range of genre-specific elements. Chart 4.2 can be used to match a variety of mentor texts with a progression of skills and strategies. Students can make their own choices when offered a selection of mentor texts, or you can use this tool to plan mentor texts for specific small groups or individual students. Therefore, we have included a column to record students' names on the right side of the chart. This column can be used for planning purposes, or to record which selections students made.

Figure 4.2 Mentor texts with charts tucked inside

In this collection of mentor texts, charts are tucked into the covers so that students can identify the skill or craft move they want to see and head to that page.

Use this tool if . . . you want to differentiate mentor texts based on accessibility and interests.

Revisit this tool . . . when planning mentor texts for new skills or genre studies.

To use this tool, you will need . . . to habitually seek new books to include in instruction.

Make this tool your own by . . . deciding whether to use it to plan different small groups or to offer mentor texts as student choices, thus recording their choices in the "Students" section.

CHART 4.2
PLANNING FOR MENTOR TEXT CHOICES

Genre: _____ Poetry _____

	MENTOR TEXT POSSIBILITIES	STUDENTS
Strategy or genre-specific component: • Imagery • Haiku • Incorporating photographs	*Seeing Into Tomorrow: Haiku* by Richard Wright (2018)	Mei, Joe, Gina, Raina, George, Carlos (small group)
Strategy or genre-specific component: • Metaphors • "I am from" style • Narrative poetry	*Where Are You From?* by Yamile Saied Méndez (2019)	Heather, Reya, Merrie, Uma, Aloki (small group)
Strategy or genre-specific component: • Rhythm • Repetition • Rhyme • Pop-out words/text that matches meaning • Shape poem • List poem	*Hip Hop Speaks to Children: A Celebration of Poetry With a Beat* by Nikki Giovanni (2008)	Jack, Kirsten, Kyle, Amaya, Keyvan, Maggie (small group)

online resources 🔍 Available for download at **resources.corwin.com/responsivewritingteacher.**

SELECTING MENTOR TEXTS FOR LINGUISTIC RESPONSIVENESS

Linguistic Responsiveness
↓
Select mentor texts that . . .
Provide support for processing, especially in multilingual texts
Contain support for language, such as labels, repetition, illustrations, definitions, or captions

"They leave the dough to rise. Amy keeps an eye on it, just in case. It grows bigger . . . and bigger . . . and even *bigger*," students read, with glee. It was the third time they had read Kat Zhang's (2019) *Amy Wu and the Perfect Bao* as a class. By this time, children knew the book well, had engaged in a baking project themselves, and were ready to study it as writers.

The repetitive, playful nature of both the text and illustrations make this a memorable, accessible, and treasured story. When searching for a mentor text such as this one, linguistic responsiveness involves looking closely at the processing and language supports that the author/illustrator have already incorporated in the text. Further responsiveness can occur in our instruction, where additional supports can be implemented for processing and developing language.

Providing Supports for Processing

When planning supports for a mentor text, it's important to keep in mind that students need to process the content *and* the text features. Reading the mentor text as a read aloud several times before studying it as writers allows children to process the content before diving into more complex details in the craft. Additional support for comprehension can be offered to students, as a whole class or in a small group, by doing the following:

- Building background knowledge of the content (through a conversation, visuals, or a video clip)
- Previewing new vocabulary
- Reading the text an additional time before/after the lesson

Language processing, in the context of a mentor text, involves the way children process and understand the author's use of words to communicate ideas and feelings. With this in mind, plan to stop and support processing anytime the author is describing a big idea or big feeling, especially when those messages are conveyed with higher-level or content-specific vocabulary.

Selecting mentor texts that are multilingual broadens the experience students have with exploring author's voice. In classrooms with students who speak additional home languages, this also allows them to be represented, linguistically, as a mentor in literature. For students who are monolingual this provides an opportunity to use context and illustration to make sense of multilingual texts and become familiar with more languages. For example, in the collection *In Daddy's Arms I Am Tall*, Javaka Steptoe (2013) includes poems written in African American Vernacular English (AAVE), which opens the possibility for students who speak AAVE as a home language to include it in their writing. For students who do not speak AAVE, it sends the message that all languages are valuable and worth learning from.

Tip for Tomorrow

When reading a multilingual book to students, authenticity is critical and delivery matters. If a book incorporates language that you are not familiar with, seek a colleague or community member who is, and ask if they are willing to join the class for read aloud. Another option is to search social media or YouTube for authors or people who speak the language reading the book on a video, then showing that to students. Students often get excited and proud to teach about or read books that incorporate their home language(s).

Children, like adults, process in different ways. Offering a variety of modalities for processing time can support a range of learning styles. Examples are provided in Figure 4.3.

Figure 4.3 Processing Supports During the Read Aloud of a Mentor Text

Support	Description	Processing-Related Example
Think aloud	The teacher shares their thinking aloud to the class.	"Hmm . . . that's a word I've never heard before/this must be a word in a language I don't know yet, called _____. I'm going to look at the pictures and read the rest of the sentence. Ahh . . . _____ must be another word for _____. I'm going to try using that word in my writing too!"
Turn and talk	Partners are given a prompt to turn and talk to each other.	"What do you think the author meant by [line from text that shows feelings or theme/big idea]? Turn and talk about it with a partner."
Act it out	Students act like a character or show what is happening with movement.	"The author just described important steps for [doing something]. I'm going to read it again while you act out the steps."
Turn and act	Partners act a part or process together, either simultaneously or through role-playing.	"Partner A is going to be [name character], and Partner B is going to be [name character]. Turn and act with each other to show what just happened/to show how you are each feeling."
Think to yourself	Students are given a prompt to think about individually.	"Make a movie in your mind. Think about what just happened, and picture what might happen next."
Think and sketch/jot	Students are invited to sketch or write their ideas in a journal or whiteboard.	"The poet just described _____. I'm going to read it again. Sketch or write about what you are picturing."
Choice	Students make a choice before the read aloud begins, or at the end of a read aloud, and can sit in a designated spot with students who are making similar choices.	"In this book, the author teaches all about [name topic]. While we read, we will stop to show what we are learning. If you prefer to act what we learn, sit here. If you prefer to jot or sketch, get a whiteboard/journal and sit here. If you prefer to talk with a partner, sit here."

After students show understanding of the content, an additional read aloud can take place in which the text becomes a *mentor,* and the teacher guides students in reading as *writers.* While doing so, to support language processing, provide oral and/or written definitions and visuals for any text features, visuals, and genre-specific elements that are studied. This can be done by co-constructing a chart while reading or annotating the text with sticky notes. These can be referenced by students as they attempt such work in their own writing. Figure 4.4 shows an example of this in a kindergarten classroom.

Figure 4.4 Charts Co-Constructed to Provide Processing Supports

This resource area displays co-constructed annotations of a mentor—*Bones,* by Steve Jenkins (2010)—alongside student mentors.

Looking Closely at Language

Grammatical structure is the way words and phrases are arranged in a sentence. Grammatical structure can range from simple to complex in literature. Books become more linguistically accessible when authors incorporate labels, repetition, or grammatical structure in engaging and meaningful ways. Labels are an especially powerful processing support for students. When books include patterns or repetition, invite children to join in your reading. Labels and patterns are also accessible craft moves for children to try in their own writing.

More complex grammatical structures include question-answer format, compound sentences, and intentional fragments. As students are developing language skills, it's helpful to provide opportunities to *notice* nuances of language, so that they can learn, understand, and use language in increasingly sophisticated ways.

Tip for Tomorrow

Though it can be challenging to find books with labels, you can add them, or children can add their own through interactive writing, especially labels that will help grow vocabulary or build meaning.

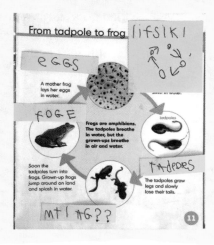

When selecting mentor texts, consider the following questions:

- Are there labels within the text that align with pictures and enrich vocabulary development?
- Does the text contain repetition that provides opportunities for practice?
- Is there accessible vocabulary that develops what students already know?
- Are there grammatical structures that are at a level at which students can note, emulate, and approximate?

It's All About Me-ow, by Hudson Talbott (2012), is a text that can serve as a mentor for information writing, and it has a variety of structures as well as labels that build vocabulary and understanding. The humorous style makes the book one that children want to return to. For example, the first page contains several questions, an important linguistic concept, as well as exclamations and a variety of punctuation. Later pages of *It's All About Me-ow* contain labels. The humor in the labels lends itself to linguistic interpretations.

Chart 4.3 serves as a template for considering language as a factor in selecting mentor texts. It may not be possible to find books that address all concepts, but the process of selecting books with this tool helps increase our awareness of language structures and ways to develop vocabulary. While we find it helpful to use sticky notes as markers in books to remind us of specific items to point out in each reading, this chart helps us grow our collection of language-oriented books throughout the year and is a tool to consider anytime we add a new book to our classroom library. That way, the chart becomes a powerful reference tool when working with multilingual students. Any time this tool is used, it can be tucked inside of the book to reference when revisiting it.

Use this tool if . . . you have students who are learning English or developing their language skills.

Revisit this tool . . . when you are searching for mentor texts, as you might notice structures and features within a text that you may otherwise overlook.

To use this tool, you will need . . . to seek mentor texts that offer creative grammatical structures, labeling, or ways to build vocabulary to add to your collection.

Make this tool your own by . . . keeping it inside mentor texts to reference when using the book again.

CHART 4.3

LINGUISTIC FUNCTIONING MENTOR TEXT TEMPLATE

Unit: Personal Narrative

Genre: Narrative

Birdsong by Julie Flett (2019)

STRUCTURES THAT BUILD LANGUAGE SKILLS	PLACES TO HIGHLIGHT OR REINFORCE IN MENTOR TEXT
Grammatical structures *Sentence structures, phrases, repetitions* Multiple reads of the same page lead to analysis of word choice and sentence structure as well as a deeper understanding of parts of speech	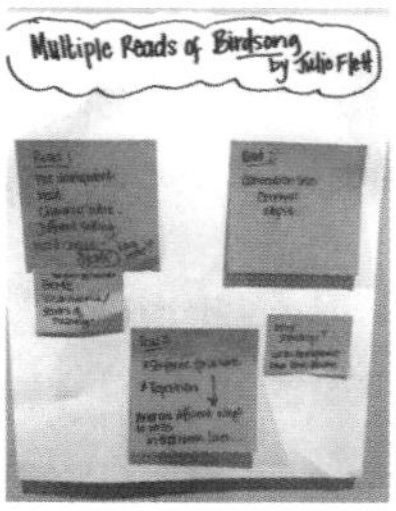
Vocabulary development *Definitions or visuals for higher-level vocabulary* Julie's use of the word *home* invites a conversation or debate around the meaning of home. Additionally, the snowdrops in the yard could lead to an exploration of other types of flowers found in yards.	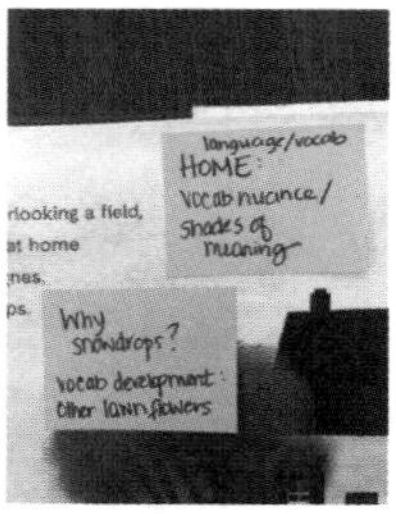
Labels *Labels or captions that help build vocabulary and understanding* Many pages in *Birdsong* offer opportunities to add labels with children to build vocabulary.	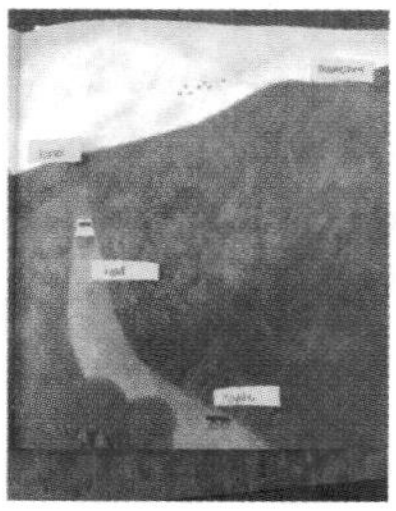

SELECTING MENTOR TEXTS FOR CULTURAL RESPONSIVENESS

Madeleine gathered a small group of children in the classroom library for an unveiling of newly filled shelves. Excitement was palpable as topical nonfiction bins were showcased that aligned with recent interests. Then, Madeleine uncovered a new bin in the mentor author section, alongside class favorites—Javaka Steptoe, Ezra Jack Keats, Grace Lin, Taro Gomi, and Rachel Isadora.

Cultural Responsiveness ↓
Select mentor texts that . . .
Include mirrors and windows for students within the authorship, content, text, and illustrations
Prioritize representation for those who have been historically underrepresented within the literacy world

"We've been reading and learning about Donald Crews. We thought we should make a special bin so that we can always find his books. Here is Donald Crews's name, and this is a picture of him," Madeleine shared, as she pointed to the label at the front of the bin.

Ethan's eyes lit up as he cradled the bin in his arms and exclaimed, "That's what Donald Crews looks like? He's my favorite author!"

Any time a book is highlighted as a mentor, not only will it represent what a genre looks like, but it also will represent what an author looks like. So it's important to ask, "What image of an author am I portraying in the selection of this text?"

In thinking about the images of authors that kindergartners, including Ethan, would be forming from the books highlighted in her classroom, Madeleine reflected:

I would like for every mentor text we center to represent a group that is traditionally underrepresented in literature. That's not because there aren't good stories about white people or forest animals. But, for most of the students, for the rest of their lives, those are the stories that will be represented as literature, and as authors. I hope that will change, but in case it doesn't, at least this year, that pattern is broken.

Cultural responsiveness, when selecting mentors for a community of writers, involves looking carefully at the representation within the text and in the creation of the text. When doing so, it's important to consider who it reflects within the classroom community, within the larger community, and within the world.

Including Mirrors and Windows for Students

Rudine Sims Bishop (1990) introduced the concept of mirrors and windows in literature. She emphasized the importance of children seeing their own lives—race, language and dialect, family structure, gender, religion, ability, class, and nationality—reflected in literature (mirrors) as well as the lives beyond their own (windows).

Figure 4.5 shows tools teachers have used to guide students with reading through the lens of mirrors and windows.

Figure 4.5

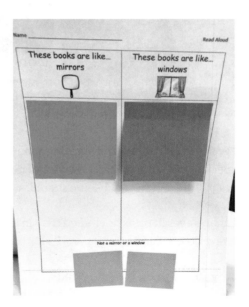

A class uses a tool to reflect on aspects of a text that are like mirrors and windows (left). A student uses a tool to record books that are like mirrors, windows, or neither (right).

During her presentation at NCTE 2019, Sonja Cherry-Paul expanded on Bishop's work, addressing the need for historically marginalized people to be represented in everyday life with conflicts that aren't related to their marginalization. Cherry-Paul and Dana Johansen (2019) also suggested thinking about representation, context, authorship, and content when selecting culturally relevant books.

Figures 4.6 and 4.7 show how teachers have taken inventory of and analyzed the representation in books, in order to plan for instruction.

Figure 4.6

From a study of representation in books, staff at PS 59 in NYC created a shared library to pull from when seeking inclusive texts.

Figure 4.7

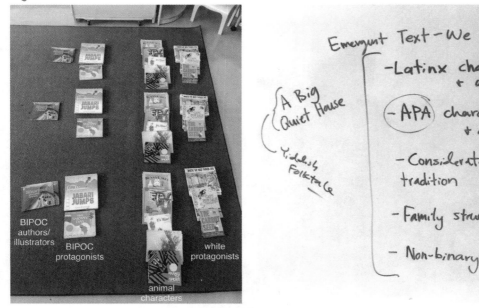
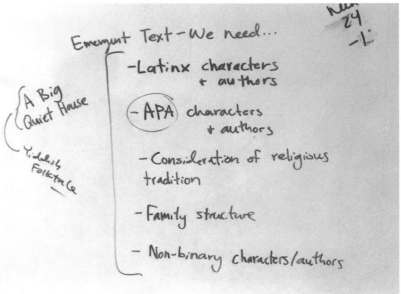

Teachers sorted books provided for a new unit. They used this data to guide their search for greater representation in texts, based on class-culturally responsive information gathered.

Educator Chad Everett (2018) nudges educators further in "Beyond Our Shelves," from his blog, *ImagineLit*, where he writes the following:

> If we stop at the presence of *diverse* literature on our shelves, we have missed the point. I fear that some of us have approached acquiring literature that accurately represents individuals from marginalized groups, like going out and looking for _insert marginalized group_ friends…. Lean in, if you have accurate representation in your library, but not in your curriculum and life, you may be reducing texts to your _insert marginalized group_ friends.

The decisions we make within classrooms matter as much as the decisions we make in the world. Though this book focuses primarily on the in-classroom work, a few of the questions that guide us in the world include:

- Who am I learning from, and how are they being compensated for their labor?
- Who is portrayed in and/or making the literature, art, and media I consume?
- How am I interacting with and contributing to my community and students' communities?

By keeping these questions at the forefront of our mind each day, we can come to know ourselves, students, neighbors, and how the choices we make either dismantle or perpetuate systems of oppression within our own spheres of influence, as demonstrated by the graphic in Figure 4.8.

Figure 4.8 Spheres of Influence

Chart 4.4 can help you closely examine the books you plan to use as mentor texts so you can ensure the books children read reflect their lives and experiences in an authentic way.

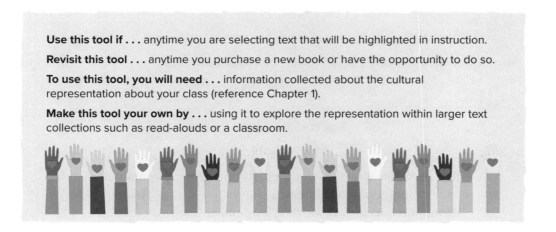

Use this tool if . . . anytime you are selecting text that will be highlighted in instruction.

Revisit this tool . . . anytime you purchase a new book or have the opportunity to do so.

To use this tool, you will need . . . information collected about the cultural representation about your class (reference Chapter 1).

Make this tool your own by . . . using it to explore the representation within larger text collections such as read-alouds or a classroom.

CHART 4.4

CONSIDERING REPRESENTATION, CONTEXT, AUTHORSHIP, AND CONTENT IN MENTOR TEXTS

GRAPHIC NOVEL/*MARCH* BY JOHN LEWIS, ANDREW AYDIN, AND NATE POWELL (2016)	

Representation:
 	
Are characters doing everyday things?
 	
Are they portrayed as victims?
 	
Is there a savior?
 	
• Black people
• Activists
• Children/child's perspective
• People living in the rural South (Alabama)
• People living in cities (mostly DC)
• People living in poverty
• Educators
• Civil rights leaders (John Lewis, Martin Luther King Jr.)
• White people (minorly)
	Context:
	
	What are people doing?
	
	Are they doing it in present time?
	
	Not just in history?
	
	• Modes of activism (boycotts, marches, sit-ins)
	• Racism
	• Jim Crow laws
	  • What they were, what life was like growing up in rural Alabama during that time for a Black family
	• Civil rights movement
	  • Major people involved, significant moments in the movement's history, accomplishments

Content: Who is the author? What makes the author uniquely positioned to tell the story? • Text used mainly to highlight the different tools that graphic novelists use to tell stories • Examples of graphic novel vocabulary, such as internal and external dialogue, caption, and image	**Authorship:** Does the text have an authentic voice? Will students want to read this book? • John Lewis, one of the key figures of the civil rights movement, telling his own story • Andrew Aydin, policy adviser to Lewis, active in social justice as well • Nate Powell, self-published, award-winning cartoonist

Source: Chart adapted from Cherry-Paul and Johansen (2019).

 Available for download at **resources.corwin.com/responsivewritingteacher.**

Tip for Tomorrow

When going through classroom or school libraries, you are likely to find books with unauthentic, stereotypical, or problematic language and text. When this happens at Compass Charter School in Brooklyn, books are taken to the "Decolonizing Compass Box." These books can then become studied by staff and/or upper-grade students to notice problematic features. In the same shared space, there is a Black Lives Matter library, where staff and students can check out books—organized from picture books to young adult (YA), and by topic, as needed for classroom study.

Prioritizing Representation

In "On Becoming an Anti-Racist Teacher of Young Writers," on the *Two Writing Teachers* blog, Kelsey posed the question that she and her coteacher, Madeleine, grounded their practice with:

How do we create a literary world in the classroom that centers authors who have historically been silenced, unrecognized, or underrepresented? By *silenced*, we think of authors whose work may never be published. By *unrecognized*, we think of authors whose work is not yet prioritized in classrooms or bookstores. By *underrepresented*, we think of authors who are not yet visible in the literacy world.

The Cooperative Children's Book Center (2020), of the University of Wisconsin, shares yearly statistics on representation in literature. The results of 2019 illustrate the disparity, both in representation and authorship, between racial groups:

- There are 5.7 percent of books by and 12.2 percent of books about individuals who are Black or African.
- Less than 1 percent of books are by and 1.2 percent of books are about First or Native Nations.
- There are 10.3 percent of books by and 9 percent of books about Asians, Asian Americans, and Pacific Islanders.
- There are 6.1 percent of books by and 6.3 percent about Latinx populations.

From this data, we can see the necessity to grow structures and systems in our classrooms that ensure Black, Indigenous, and peoples of color (BIPOC) are seen, heard, and celebrated as writers, by doing the following:

- Curating a collection of books in a classroom library, displaying books that children should see displayed in bookstores and libraries
- Highlighting authors as mentors to children—authors who should be considered mentors to all
- Coauthoring books with children—books that children should see more of in the world
- Creating systems and structures within writing workshops that prioritize access and equity to BIPOC—systems and structures that should be the norm

In making such commitments, change begins at a classroom microlevel, feeding the larger movement against systemic oppression in literature. In making and naming the process of such commitments during instruction, children can become equipped to seek representative mentors and voices within and beyond the classroom.

Tip for Tomorrow

Many authors have shared videos of themselves reading their books on YouTube and their social media accounts. Watching these in classrooms can help students feel more connected to authors. It also offers an important opportunity for students to see and listen to authors of color read their own books. Watching these videos shifts mentorship from just the texts to the authors as well.

Another way to represent students as authors and illustrators is to include students' work alongside the work of mentors. Some teachers have done this with samples of writing, where students have tried the same strategies as mentors. Other teachers include photographs or quotes of children who are trying the work. Figures 4.9 and 4.10 show classrooms in which student work is highlighted alongside published books.

Figure 4.9

This teacher includes a box of student-published books on the shelves alongside mentor authors, sending the message that children are authors too.

Figure 4.10

This classroom resource area features one column of annotated work by "World Authors," alongside another column of "Class Authors," honoring both approximation and representation of students.

SELECTING MENTOR TEXTS FOR SOCIAL-EMOTIONAL RESPONSIVENESS

In a recorded interview, Roda Ahmed (author of *Mae Among the Stars* [2018]) asked author Nikkolas Smith, "What inspired you to write?"

Smith replied, "When I was younger, I drew X-Men and cars and Looney Tunes. I'd try to re-create what I saw on TV. I was always drawing. I think it was the realization that I can add so much more depth to the art if I have a backstory or layers to the character, and so sometimes I would add little notes or characteristics of the people I was drawing. I decided I wanted my art to become a book one day."

When referencing encouragement Smith has received as a writer, he added, "Someone told me, if you stop [writing], who's going to be able to tell the story from your specific perspective? I am definitely going to keep going. I'm going to keep making more stories and more art every week."

After reading his book *The Golden Girls of Rio* with Ahmed, Smith (2016) shared one of the central messages he hopes the book sends to children: "It's not about how fast or strong you are, but what you do with your power."

Smith's interests, purpose, and habits as a writer are visible in his work and in this interview. Social-emotional responsiveness, when it comes to mentor texts, involves inviting students in on the writerly lives of authors and illustrators.

Social-Emotional Responsiveness ↓
Select mentor texts that . . .
Match relevant topics and/or interests of students with topics and story lines in the mentor texts
Incorporate social-emotional support and/or positive habits of mind

Matching Relevant Topics and/or Interests of Students to Mentor Texts

Mentor texts require close and repeated readings. When students relate to and show interest in the content, they will be more apt to revisit those texts, thereby increasing the positive impacts of having a mentor. The following questions can be used when determining the potential level of student engagement with a mentor text, or when searching for a mentor text that can engage a class or small group of students.

Genre of Focus	Guiding Questions to Determine Level of Student Engagement
Personal narrative	Can students connect with the characters, setting, and story line? Are there conflicts that students have experienced in their own lives—within or outside of school?
Informational	Do students show interest and/or inquiry in the topic(s) of focus, within or outside of school?
Opinion	Does the focus align with needs and problems that are relevant to students' lives, within the school and larger communities?
Procedural	Does the text demonstrate a skill that students have shown interest in acquiring?
Poetry	Will the style, topic, emotion, and/or rhythm of the poem captivate students' attention?

Promoting Positive Habits of Mind

Katie Wood Ray (2002) writes, in *What You Know by Heart*, "I often think that when I watch a really good teacher of writing, it's almost like there are life-size cardboard cutouts of authors all around the room. Jane Yolen is standing up by the chalkboard and Eloise Greenfield is just by the door to welcome students as they enter.... With a room full of authors to help us, teaching writing doesn't have to be so lonely" (p. 150).

There are a number of ways to bring authors and illustrators to life in classrooms. Doing so is an important way to build trust and inspiration that bring life to a mentorship. It also adds authenticity to instruction, as young writers can see the skills they are developing present in books they hold. When it comes to overcoming obstacles as a writer and developing positive habits of mind, this is especially important.

Here are some ways to bring authors to life for your students:

1. Read the biography in the back of a book, which frequently includes a photograph.

2. Interview the author. Some teachers help students send questions to authors on social media or via email/mail. Many authors are willing to do visits with school, in person, or via videoconferencing. Students can prepare questions ahead of time.

3. Search interviews and videos authors/illustrators post on their social media accounts, websites, and YouTube. Many share personal stories, challenges, and strategies about their process.

Tip for Tomorrow

To foster students' writing identities, try the following:

- Use students' first names in combination with authors' first names, building recognition that students *and* authors can be mentors! For example, if Jacqueline Woodson is a favorite classroom author, then say something along the lines of "Jacqueline and _____ (fill in student's name) both use _____ in their writing."
- Notice and name when students are attempting craft moves and text elements that were studied in a mentor text: "You (name text element or craft move) just like (author/ illustrator) did!"
- In charts, in demonstrations, or in share sessions, show how students *and* authors have used a craft move within their writing.

The content of books can also help students with navigating the complex challenges they face, leveraging the power of mentor texts in positive ways. Such challenges may be present in school, outside of school, or within the writing process itself. By thinking about problems that are relevant for a class of students, a small group of students, or an individual student, responsive selections of mentor texts can be made.

During the first reading(s) of a mentor text, when the focus is comprehension, we can do the following:

1. Notice the challenge faced or posed.

2. Notice the strategies of a growth mindset.

3. Notice solutions.

4. Provide time for student talk, during and after the read aloud. This can be a time for them to connect to the challenge, or generate ideas for coping with such a challenge.

Gaia Cornwell's (2020) *Jabari Jumps* illustrates optimism and strategies for releasing fear.

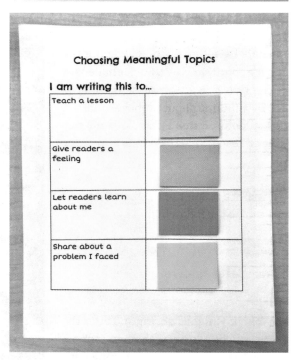

Mentor texts were selected to portray how authors can write about meaningful topics, then students can think of their own meaningful ideas.

Responsive Mentor Texts Across the Domains

While this book is structured so that each domain can be returned to when focusing on any given area of responsiveness, the domains are not mutually exclusive. Here, we share a classroom example of how academic, linguistic, cultural, and social-emotional responsiveness become integrated in instruction.

Putting It in Practice

From Brekke McDowell, an upper-elementary teacher:

As students enter upper-level elementary grades, there is a shift, and much of the focus becomes argument essay writing. It's hard to find authentic mentor texts for this! I've found that the most authentic mentor texts for this mode of writing comes from previous students.

There are important questions I consider when selecting an "authentic" mentor text. The first is this: Does this mentor serve as a real example of what a child in my class could write? When writing an opinion piece, showing an op-ed from the *New York Times* may work, but often the language or topics discussed don't match students' interests and current understanding of that genre of writing.

The second question to consider is this: Does the author of this mentor text challenge the biases prevalent in the publishing world? This means decentering white authors and creating space for students to study the works of Black, brown, and Indigenous authors. This also means challenging the idea that only adults are authors. When students study the works of their peers and classmates, it shows that they are authors too!

To select student mentor texts, I look back at old examples from previous years (saved on Google Classroom or others that were handwritten I save in my desk). I always ask the writer's permission to include it. Many students would recognize the mentor author's name when reading and learning from them (Example: "Oh, I know Maya! She's a seventh grader now!"). Including mentor texts from former students offers students a mirror to see themselves and their classmates as writers also worthy of reading and learning from.

Digging Deeper

Throughout the chapter, we referenced specific resources. To read more about any of these concepts, we recommend the following books and resources:

- *Craft Moves: Lesson Sets for Teaching Writing With Mentor Texts* by Stacey Shubitz (2016)

- *Mentor Texts: Teaching Writing Through Children's Literature, K–6* by Lynne Dorfman and Rose Cappelli

- *In Pictures and In Words: Teaching the Qualities of Good Writing Through Illustration Study* by Katie Wood Ray (2010)

- *Learning From Classmates: Using Students' Writing as Mentor Texts* by Lisa Eickholdt (2015)

- *What You Know by Heart: How to Develop Curriculum for Your Writing Workshop* by Katie Wood Ray (2002)

Tip for Tomorrow

A growing number of resources are available for growing inclusive classroom libraries:

- **#Ownvoices:** In 2015, Corinne Duyvis coined the term *#ownvoices*, in which "the protagonist and the author share a marginalized identity" (http://www.corinneduyvis.net/ownvoices/).
- *School Library Journal:* **"A Diversity & Cultural Literacy Toolkit":** Recommended resources, articles, videos for cultural literacy (Parrott, 2018; https://www.slj.com/?detailStory=diversity-cultural-literacy-toolkit)
- **We Need Diverse Books:** A nonprofit organization that advocates for changes in the publishing industry to produce and promote literature that reflects and honors the lives of all young people (https://diversebooks.org/)
- **Teaching Tolerance:** A website that provides free resources for educators, promoting the development of children and youth to be active participants in a diverse democracy (https://www.tolerance.org/about)
- **Social Justice Books:** A guide and resource for selecting anti-bias children's books (https://socialjusticebooks.org/booklists/)
- **We Are Kid Lit Collective:** Works to create materials and opportunities to recognize the humanity of Black, Indigenous, and peoples of color (BIPOC) in youth literature (https://wtpsite.com)
- **Diverse Book Finder:** Includes collections of books featuring BIPOC characters, search tools, critical data, and collection analysis tool to use when analyzing and curating libraries and book collections (https://diversebookfinder.org)
- **Classroom Library Questionnaire:** An interactive tool from Lee & Low Books to help you analyze your classroom library and determine where there are strengths and gaps in representation (https://www.leeandlow.com/educators/grade-level-resources/classroom-library-questionnaire)

Tool for Planning Across the Domains

Mentor Texts

This tool can be used as a place to take notes, reflect, or expand upon the ideas in this chapter. Alternatively, it can also be used to plan for responsiveness across the domains.

Academic Responsiveness	Linguistic Responsiveness
• *Accessible to students as readers and writers* • *Text elements and craft moves that students can approximate*	• *Support for processing, especially in multilingual texts* • *Support for language (e.g., labels, captions, visuals, definitions)*

Cultural Responsiveness	Social-Emotional Responsiveness
• *Identities and experiences familiar and unfamiliar to students*	• *Matched interests and/or relevant topics* • *Incorporation of social-emotional support or positive habits of mind*

online resources ↘ Available for download at **resources.corwin.com/responsivewritingteacher.**

CHAPTER 5

Providing Responsive Demonstration Texts

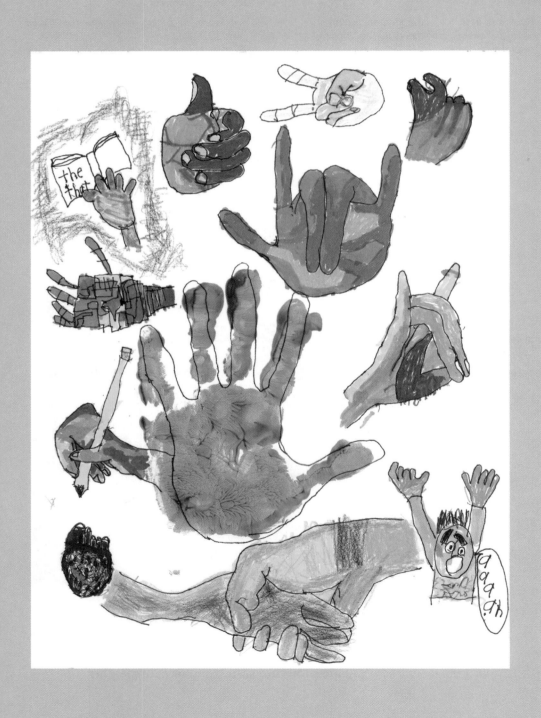

Through texts and writerly processes, educators model the craft moves, decision-making, and self-talk of authors at work. Demonstration texts that are intentional and explicit keep students at the forefront—representing, engaging, inspiring, and inviting young writers in along the way.

Rasha Hamid, who has taught in Sudan, East Harlem, Hamilton Heights, and Brooklyn, is a creator: a talented artist, musician, and chef. She weaves each of these into her literacy instruction. Rasha is also a writer. She writes for educators; she writes songs, poems, and letters of activism. Rasha writes books for children, in front of children, and with children—demonstrating both the writing process and habits of a writerly life:

> I was teaching in Khartoum. I asked my second graders, what do you picture when you think of Sudan? They said it was dry, dusty, dirty, hot, and ugly. I thought, *What about Sudan's mountains, rivers and fields?* I looked for books to show them, but I couldn't find any.

That year, Christopher Myers, author and illustrator, came to visit our class. His book, *Black Cat*, was one of our favorites, illustrated with photos of his Brooklyn neighborhood. He talked to us about powerful writing and told us home is that earth-shaking place! So we wrote about home.

When we were done, we had a stunning book celebrating Sudan, filled with information children had gathered during our study, co-created by every member of our class, with translations (to Sudanese Arabic, French, Spanish, Korean and Japanese) and images provided by families and other members of our school community. (Indiegogo, n.d.)

That book written with children in Rasha's classroom inspired a published book, *Kadisa* كديسة *: A Journey Through Sudan* (Hamid, 2017), told in English and Sudanese-Arabic. *Kadisa* كديسة is one of the very few picture books available for young children about Sudan.

Many things were demonstrated in the process of writing *Kadisa* كديسة—making a book that is needed in the world, finding inspiration in a writerly mentor, and creating a poetic informative text in addition to collaborative writing, translation, community involvement, and the process of publishing.

Why Demonstration Texts Matter

We encourage educators to immerse in two (or more!) writing practices—one that mirrors what students are writing throughout the year and one that is a personal writing of choice. For example, Kelsey has notebooks tucked around her home for sketching, journaling, and writing poetry, and Melanie returns to her series of young adult (YA) fiction writing when outside the classroom. In this chapter, we focus on writing that is used in instruction: demonstration writing.

Donald Graves and Penny Kittle have long voiced the importance of writing alongside students. In their book *Inside Writing: How to Teach the Details of Craft,* Graves and Kittle (2005) explain, "Today's teachers are pressed for time is a gross understatement. Nevertheless, when teachers compose texts of their own—texts they care about—during writing workshop, precious time is saved. Teachers reveal to their students the decisions all writers must make about every aspect of writing and demonstrate the skills that make writing clear and meaningful" (p. 1).

Within a demonstration text, we can model specific skills, strategies, or text elements of study. Beyond a text, we can model *so much more* as writers—voicing the messy process it entails, that ideas and words are at times plentiful and at times sparse, that some drafts get abandoned, that certain genres offer solace when lost, that fuel can be found in the words of others, and that written and spoken words serve many purposes. Educators who write grow empathy, authenticity, connectedness, expertise, effectiveness, and responsiveness—ultimately talking and thinking like a writer, as illustrated in Figure 5.1.

Figure 5.1 Educators Who Write, Grow

Tip for Tomorrow

Keep your own writing folder that matches and is placed alongside student writing folders. Though you might prefer keeping texts that are specifically for demonstrations with other instructional materials, keeping recently written texts in a folder shows students that you are writing alongside them. More ways to do this include the following:

- Pick one day each week to spend the first or final few minutes of independent writing time engaging in the same kind of writing students are doing. Consider it a live demonstration writing time to model certain skills (you can even name them!), as they will likely be curious to see what you are working on.
- Write alongside students for five to ten minutes during choice times throughout the day, such as during a soft start or playtime.

When considering the creation and use of demonstration texts in responsive instruction, we are reminded of Toni Morrison's words: "If there's a book that you want to read, but it hasn't been written yet, then you must write it." We are book collectors, constantly on the search for new titles to inspire young writers. However, each year, we are reminded that no text aligns with students as much as one that has been written with them specifically in mind. For the same reasons that we modify or re-create existing charts and seek new mentors, we also write fresh demonstration texts with each class: ones that respond to a specific group of students.

Different Types of Demonstration Writing

We have separated the chapters about mentor texts and demonstration texts, even though there is some overlap between them. While mentor texts (see Chapter 4) are typically published works that can be studied and approximated, demonstration texts are written intentionally and specifically for teaching traits and craft moves within a genre. Although mentor texts are typically far beyond what students can produce, demonstration texts are representative of work that students can do. Finally, while mentor texts are typically a finished product, demonstration texts allow students to see within the drafting process.

There are several types of demonstration texts. Before deciding upon any type, it's important to start with purpose, as with any tool. Demonstration texts can model the structure and elements of a genre, a specific strategy, or the development of a skill as it increases with complexity. Different kinds of demonstration texts can be created and utilized for each of these purposes, as outlined in Figure 5.2.

Figure 5.2 Types of Demonstration Texts

Exemplar demonstration text	This models elements of a genre that align with unit, grade level, or student-specific goals.

Sticky notes mark text features demonstrated in this exemplar text.

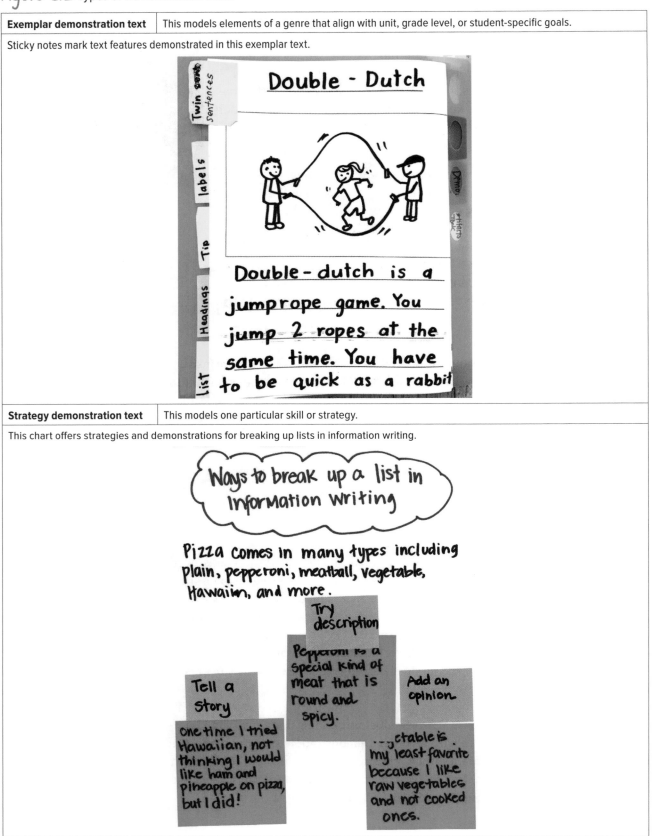

Strategy demonstration text	This models one particular skill or strategy.

This chart offers strategies and demonstrations for breaking up lists in information writing.

Progression demonstration texts	One text, or portion of a text, is written several times with increasing levels of complexity. Provide various entry points and incremental pathways for growth of a specific skill or strategy.

This text shows three beginnings, increasing in complexity, for a story. Students or teachers can name the differences in the space that follows.

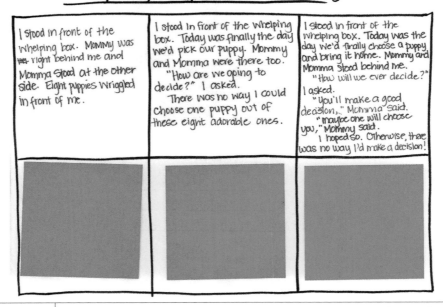

Creating a beginning for a narrative story

Panel 1: I stood in front of the whelping box. Mommy was right behind me and Momma stood at the other side. Eight puppies wriggled in front of me.

Panel 2: I stood in front of the whelping box. Today was finally the day we'd pick our puppy. Mommy and Momma were there too. "How are we going to decide?" I asked. There was no way I could choose one puppy out of these eight adorable ones.

Panel 3: I stood in front of the whelping box. Today was the day we'd finally choose a puppy and bring it home. Mommy and Momma stood behind me. "How will we ever decide?" I asked. "You'll make a good decision," Momma said. "Maybe one will choose you," Mommy said. I hoped so. Otherwise, there was no way I'd make a decision!

Co-created demonstration texts	Skills are demonstrated and practiced with students in the co-creation of a text. This can be done through shared writing (students plan, teacher scribes) or interactive writing (co-planning, co-scribing).

We walked to Thor's foster home. He was waiting for us at the door!

☐ who ☐ what ☐ where ☐ how

Through interactive writing, students demonstrated how to show feelings in a story (shown in purple).

(Continued)

(Continued)

These types of demonstration texts are not mutually exclusive. For example, an exemplar text can be rewritten with increasing levels of complexity, forming a progression. A strategy demonstration text can be co-created. Using a text for multiple purposes can be beneficial, as the more familiar a text is to students, the more the learner can study the craft moves within the piece.

This exemplar for a procedural text was co-constructed through shared writing.

With the exception of exemplar pieces, we recommend resisting the urge to have one piece do everything; too much information runs the risk of being overwhelming. Additionally, while exemplar texts contain examples of many elements and features, they should stay within grade-level benchmarks that align with students' skills and goals. That way, students have a piece to aim for that is within their zone of proximal development (ZPD). (For more about ZPDs, see Chapter 2.)

Deciding which kind of demonstration text to use for a specific class or small group of students is one way to be responsive. Further responsiveness occurs when demonstration texts build upon developing skills, support language development, and are reflective of identities and interests. Our hope is that this chapter encourages and empowers you to create and use your own writing for demonstration.

Academic Responsiveness ↓	Linguistic Responsiveness ↓	Cultural Responsiveness ↓	Social-Emotional Responsiveness ↓
Provide demonstration texts that...			
Model skills that students are developing Provide multiple entry points for developing specific skills	Mirror the structure and length of sentences students can produce Support vocabulary development through the use of definitions, visuals, and/or labels	Authentically portray the identities and experiences that are familiar and unfamiliar to students	Align with student interests and reflect shared experiences Model social-emotional skills and positive habits of mind in content or writing process

ACADEMICALLY RESPONSIVE DEMONSTRATION TEXTS

At a recent professional development session with teachers of special education, Melanie instructed everyone to touch their knees, then their shins, then their toes. At that point many of the teachers groaned and exclaimed. Several of them refused to try. When Melanie asked them to keep their knees straight and place their palms on the floor, most of the teachers looked baffled at the direction and stood up without trying.

"But we ask our students to put their palms on the floor when it comes to writing all the time," Melanie said, "and then we wonder why they want to give up before they even try."

In order to become more flexible, incremental steps work to increase the reach. Just as flexibility can increase, writing skills also increase when instruction happens close to students' current abilities (within their ZPD), rather than at levels way beyond them. This is why intentional demonstration writing can sometimes be more effective than mentor texts. In the creation and use of demonstration texts, examples of skills or strategies can be explicit and intentional, making the tool accessible, responsive, and inspiring.

Academic Responsiveness ↓
Provide demonstration texts that...
Model skills that students are developing
Provide multiple entry points for developing specific skills

Modeling Skills That Students Are Developing

When deciding upon text elements and skills to model in a demonstration text, reference academic data collected (see Chapter 1) from student writing. Demonstration texts can be planned at the beginning of a new unit by looking at data from the end of the previous unit. They can also be planned as an additional support in the middle of a unit, for targeted practice of a specific skill. It's also helpful to look at applicable grade-level standards for your classroom, alongside standards for the previous and following grade. Some curriculum guides offer a progression of skills developing across the grades.

Once a targeted focus is determined, a demonstration text can be used as a model, and there are various ways to do so, as listed here:

Text features targeted skill or elements.	• In a guided-practice approach, the teacher identifies, names, and describes the areas of focus. • In an inquiry approach, students are invited to identify and reflect upon the area of focus.
Text does not feature targeted skill or elements.	• Teacher revises or edits the text in front of students, naming the focus and process. Then, students are invited to actively engage in the revisions in another part of the text. • A student models revising or editing their text in front of the class (this may take place after a 1:1 conference with a student) while the teacher supports in naming the focus and process. Students are invited to try the revisions or edits in their own writing.

Text is co-constructed with students.	• Targeted skill or text element is described prior to writing. The class practices it together in a session of shared writing or interactive writing.
	  • In shared writing, the teacher scribes the text as students compose it.
	    • Works well for practicing craft moves, such as elaboration
	  • In interactive writing, the teacher scribes most of the text, while sharing the pen at certain points of practice. Students can use whiteboards to practice at the same time.
	    • Works well for practicing the mechanics of writing—spelling, clear pictures, punctuation, spacing, etc.

Chart 5.1 can help you determine the specific skill you want to teach and plan how you'll teach it in the demonstration text.

Use this tool to ... hone in on the specific skill that you want to teach or address in your demonstration text.

Revisit this tool ... after you have assessed student writing and are planning how to create tools and differentiate instruction for specific skills and students.

To use this tool, you will need ... information collected about students (Chapter 1) and plans (Chapter 2). You can also reference previously made demonstration text or ones provided by curriculum.

Make this tool your own by ... attaching it to the back of your demonstration text to reference in the future.

CHART 5.1
PLANNING A FOCUS FOR A DEMONSTRATION TEXT

Area of focus: (describe skill, standard, or text element)	Using a combination of dialogue, action, and description within a narrative text
Type of text used to demonstrate: (exemplar, strategy, or progression)	Exemplar
Will text be written with or without area of focus prior to modeling?	With
Method of modeling: (teacher/student models, guided practice, inquiry, co-constructed writing)	Teacher/student models
Draft text (or plan to include a student's text):	**Excerpt from planting radishes story** I stood back from the raised garden bed we had built next to our house. Abuela and I had been filling it with soil, and we were ready to plant some of the radish seeds. "Do you really think they will grow?" I asked. "If you plant them the right way," she said. She handed me the seed packet and showed me how to space the seeds. Then, she picked up a handful of dirt and sprinkled it over the tiny black seeds.

online resources ➤ Available for download at **resources.corwin.com/responsivewritingteacher.**

Model Skills as a Progression to Offer Multiple Entry Points

Fitness instructors often provide a series of choices for exercises. Modifications are demonstrated, which simplify or add more challenge to the workout. Practitioners choose the just-right move, based on individual goals and needs. Progressions serve a similar purpose for writing, as they model a skill in various stages of complexity and allow students to engage in the work in a way that is just-right for them. Offering progressions for skills students are working on brings academic responsiveness to instruction.

When deciding upon a skill to demonstrate across a progression, think about which skills show the greatest disparity across the class. Then, select the skill that is most relevant to current instruction.

To create a progression of demonstration texts:

1. Pick one specific skill to model. Name, describe, and/or use visuals to define the skill at the top of a chart.

2. Identify progressions or grade-level standards across several grades to understand how a skill develops.

3. Make a three-column chart to model the developing skill.

4. Decide upon one topic for the text/illustration that will be used across columns.

5. Use labels, arrows, or highlighter tape to make it clear where and how the skill is developing.

6. Try to use the same words whenever possible so students can notice, note, and try out the differences more easily.

7. Keep text as concise as possible,

8. Many progressions are labeled by stars, grade levels, or adjectives of writers/writing. Though unintentional, consider how the labels might impact students' identities and instill a competitive nature. Instead, decide whether or not labels are truly needed. Without labels, progressions can be illustrated as a path, with everyone in a different part of their journey. Stages of a progression can also be labeled by key descriptors of the skill.

Chart 5.2 can support the creation of a progression.

Use this tool if ... you are providing different entry points and pathways for students to practice specific skills.

Revisit this tool ... in new genre studies or when students are developing a skill at different pathways.

To use this tool, you will need ... to create a progression, to describe how a skill progresses (some teachers annotate or highlight to show this, other teachers engage students in guided inquiry to label skill development), then engage students with identifying where they might find their own entry point.

Make this tool your own by ... writing your own demonstration text.

CHART 5.2

DEMONSTRATING A SKILL ACROSS A PROGRESSION

Information Writing

SKILL TO DEVELOP:		
Use linking words (e.g., *because*, *and*, *also*) to connect opinion and reasons.	Use linking words and phrases (e.g., *because*, *therefore*, *since*, *for example*) to connect opinion and reasons.	Link opinion and reasons using words and phrases (e.g., *for instance*, *in order to*, *in addition*).
WRITING SAMPLES:		
Chuck E. Cheese is one of the best places to play in the world because there are so many games to choose from. Also, the people who work there are friendly and helpful.	Chuck E. Cheese is one of the best places to play in the world because there are so many games to choose from. For example, there are arcade games, dance games, prize games, and video games! Therefore, it's one of my favorite places.	Chuck E. Cheese is one of the best places to play in the world because there are so many games to choose from. For example, there are arcade games, dance games, prize games, and video games! In order to pick a prize before you leave, you have to collect tokens from playing games. Last but not least, they have THE BEST PIZZA EVER! You should go to Chuck E. Cheese now!

online resources ☞ Available for download at **resources.corwin.com/responsivewritingteacher.**

LINGUISTICALLY RESPONSIVE DEMONSTRATION TEXTS

Lulu's teacher kneeled alongside her, taking a few moments to admire the writer at work before beginning the conference. "Can you tell me about the work you are doing as a writer today?" Lulu continued to touch up the details of her illustrations and responded, "I'm writing about the time I graduated pre-K at Japanese school. These words are in Japanese, and these words are in English. I learned how to write in Japanese first. It's easier for me."

Smiling, Lulu's teacher, said, "So you wrote your sentence in Japanese first, right? Then, you wrote the same sentence in English. Which feels trickier to you." Lulu nodded. "It can be so helpful for writers to start with what they know—with things that feel easier—before something that feels tricky. That's what you did! You can do that anytime you write, or even when you're doing other things that are tricky! Start with what you know."

Lulu's teacher continued, "I'm wondering … did you know that when authors write a book in more than one language, it's called *multilingual?* You've written a multilingual book! People who speak Japanese *and* people who speak English will be able to read it." Lulu beamed. "Is it okay, Lulu, if we share how you've written in two languages that you know? We have books in our library like this, and I think you might even inspire other writers in our class to do the same thing."

Writing in multiple languages was not something that existed in grade-level standards, nor was it included in the scope and sequence for the genre study. But Lulu's teacher knew that many students in the class were multilingual and that multilingual speakers do not fully rely on one language or another. Rather, they pull from the structures of multiple languages to convey meaning, a process called *translanguaging.* Having the choice to draft in multiple languages can be beneficial.

Lulu's teacher recognized that this was a valuable and responsive learning moment. It empowered Lulu to model the process in her own demonstration text. Through the demonstration, the class had a model for persisting at something that is challenging and discovered what bilingual books are. Other multilingual speakers in the class were inspired to do the same.

Mirroring the Structure and Length of Sentences Students Can Produce

The writing in mentor texts often far exceeds writing students can produce. Building off of inspiration that the class has found in mentor texts, text elements, and craft moves can be modeled with more accessibility in demonstration texts. One way to ensure the language is accessible is to use student texts as demonstration texts. To do so, it's helpful to save exemplary student work over the years, though using current student work whenever possible is ideal. Seeing what authors their age can do is motivating and inspiring to children.

Linguistic Responsiveness ↓
Provide demonstration texts that...
Mirror the structure and length of sentences students can produce
Support vocabulary development through the use of definitions, visuals, and/or labels

When creating a teacher-made demonstration text, or planning for one that is cowritten with students, it's important to think carefully about the language(s) used. When doing so, consider the length and structure of sentences, content-specific vocabulary used, as well as the volume of text. Think about typical sentence structures often used in the genre of study and incorporate those in the demonstration text.

For whole-class demonstration texts, use language(s), sentence structures, and volume that is just beyond what the higher level of proficiency is in the class. With this said, you may decide to write demonstration texts at multiple levels of proficiency, so they are more accessible to students. These can be used in small-group instruction or in student conferences.

Demonstration texts are also an opportunity for educators and/or students to model multilingual writing, code-switching, and translanguaging, as Lulu modeled in her book. For students who are multilingual, this demonstration supports their own writing process. For students who are monolingual, this demonstration provides insight into impressive multilinguistic processes.

Supporting Vocabulary Development Through the Use of Definitions, Visuals, and/or Labels

In addition to the length, structure, and volume of sentences, demonstration texts can include and support the acquisition of content-specific vocabulary words. Vocabulary can be reinforced by providing oral and/or written definitions alongside the demonstration text, in labels or the illustrations of the text. Vocabulary can also be reinforced by writing alongside a genre-specific word wall that includes visual support for each vocabulary word, as shown in Figure 5.3.

Figure 5.3

Visuals and labels are shown on sticky notes in this demonstration text, supporting vocabulary development for *who, what,* and *where* in narrative writing.

CULTURALLY RESPONSIVE DEMONSTRATION TEXTS

Linda Kim, a teacher who writes, was searching for a book that demonstrates emotion expressions for her daughter, who is multilingual—a book that she could also use in her classroom. Linda couldn't find any books written in Korean about emotions that include children of color, so she was inspired to make and print her own.

As the author, Linda decided to name the emotion on each page and ask why someone might feel that way. Knowing skills her daughter was developing, which were parallel to the skills her students are developing, Linda created a book that supports the use of language to describe emotions, body language, and facial expressions.

This grew into a treasured book in Linda's home and classroom, where she used it to demonstrate the portrayal of emotions in narrative writing.

Demonstration texts are an opportunity to provide inclusive representation that may be difficult to find in mentor texts. Such texts can be crafted by teachers or with students and can reflect children's lives within school and in surrounding communities. Demonstration texts can also open doors to lives beyond those that are familiar to students.

Cultural Responsiveness ↓
Provide demonstration texts that...
Authentically portray the identities and experiences that are familiar and unfamiliar to students

Representing the Lives of Students Inside and Outside of School

It helps to reference information collected about students' identities (revisit tools from Chapter 1) when creating a demonstration text. In doing so, reflect on the major social identities of a classroom of students. When it comes to race, language and dialect, family structure, gender, religion, ability, class, and nationality, ask the following:

Who is most frequently represented in classroom literature?

Then, shift the spotlight on groups who have been historically silenced in literature. Demonstration texts offer opportunities for marginalized groups—most urgently, Black, Indigenous, and peoples of color (BIPOC)—to be seen, heard, and celebrated *within writing* and *as writers.*

When thinking about representation, consider *who* to feature in your text, *what* the text will be about, and *where* the text will take place. Then, think about how these elements will be portrayed: Will they perpetuate or expunge stereotypes? Figure 5.4 shows an example from a primary-grade classroom discussing informational text.

Figure 5.4 Demonstration Text for Informational Text

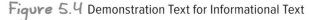

Demonstration texts, which also dispel gender norms, were co-constructed during an information genre study.

As much as representation matters, *authentic representation* matters more. Study student writing and drawings, co-create drawings with them, ask for photographs from families (with permission), lean on colleagues and community members and mentor texts, immerse in student neighborhoods, listen to the music students listen to, watch the shows they talk about, play the games they play, *listen to their stories.*

Chart 5.3 can be used as a guide for planning a culturally responsive demonstration text, with a focus on the content and illustrations.

Use this tool if ... you are planning a culturally responsive demonstration text for a specific class or small group of students.

Revisit this tool ... when crafting texts for new skills and/or genres. It might be helpful to save a completed planning tool to re-create new texts in the future.

To use this tool, you will need ... information gathered about students' cultural and social identities (revisit tools from Chapter 1) and instructional plans. It might also be helpful to reference any demonstration text(s) included in curricular plans and/or previously created demonstration texts to modify.

Make this tool your own by ... adding space to sketch/draft the demonstration text and/or annotate the text for instructional purposes. Reading a variety of texts across the genre can also help with planning the demonstration and building understanding.

CHART 5.3

PLANNING FOR CULTURAL REPRESENTATION OF DEMONSTRATION TEXTS

Genre/Demonstration Text: Grade 5, Research Paper (Informational)/Essay Written by Shawn About the 2010 Earthquake in Haiti

Notes:

- Will demonstrate how to introduce a genre (research paper)

- Will demonstrate how to zoom in on specific skills, such as building context, parenthetical citations, directly quoted evidence, writing a hook to grab the reader's attention, etc.

Guiding Questions:	Space to Plan:
When answering each question, consider race, language and dialect, family structure, gender, religion, ability, class, and nationality.	*Include plans to ensure authenticity and representation (consider illustrations, content, and language).*
Who will be featured in demonstration texts used during this genre study?	- Former student as author (representation for current students; opportunity to see other children like them as authors) - Haitian people - People living in poverty - People experiencing a natural disaster - Children activists
What topics will be featured in demonstration texts used during this genre study?	- The 2010 earthquake - The struggles of a country suffering from a national disaster without adequate funding or resources to recover - Activism or ways people can help
Where: What settings will the demonstration texts represent?	- The nation of Haiti

online resources 🔍 Available for download at **resources.corwin.com/responsivewritingteacher.**

SOCIAL-EMOTIONALLY RESPONSIVE DEMONSTRATION TEXTS

Social-Emotional Responsiveness
↓
Provide demonstration texts that...
Align with student interests and reflect shared experiences
Model social-emotional skills and positive habits of mind in content or writing process

First graders were concerned about the unkind words and actions of government leaders. As writer-activists, they decided to write a book for their community, promoting kindness and compassion. As a procedural genre study approached, their teachers leaned in to this moment as an opportunity to co-construct a text. By demonstrating the elements of a procedural text, teachers supported the class with authoring *The Kindness Book: How to Be Kind*. When it was completed, they made miniature photocopies and distributed the books around their neighborhood.

Texts can, at the same time, demonstrate a skill—such as idea generation—*and* support social-emotional development. Social-emotional responsiveness, in the context of demonstration texts, is the process of aligning the content of the text and/or instruction with student interests and social-emotional needs.

Aligning With Student Interests and Reflecting Shared Experiences

As with charts and mentor texts, demonstration texts are more engaging when they pique students' interests. This can be done in several ways, listed in the text box that follows. Figure 5.5 shows an example of a demonstration text based on a shared experience.

Ways to Make Demonstration Texts More Interesting and Engaging	
Within the content of the text	The topic of a demonstration text in an informational genre study can feature a topic that many students are interested in or curious about.
By incorporating a shared experience	The topic of a demonstration text in a procedural genre study can be written after a shared experience of making something.
Connecting to a meaningful, relevant purpose	A skill or text feature can be demonstrated that students have a meaningful need for, are showing interest in, or are experimenting with, such as lift-up flaps, dedication pages, incorporation of jokes or comics, etc.

Figure 5.5 Example of Demonstration Text Based on a Shared Experience

This demonstration text was created without punctuation to model (through guided practice) intentional choices that authors make about ending sentences. The content of the text is based on a shared experience of students.

Modeling Social-Emotional Skills and Positive Habits of Mind

Though the experiences of each student and each class of students are unique, the existence of challenging situations is not. Students are bound to encounter hard times in their lives. Whether those big moments are experienced by individual students or shared, children can lean on writing to heal. Writing-related social-emotional development can also be supported with the use of a demonstration text. Here are some examples of how this can be done:

Examples of Nonwriting-Related Social-Emotional Skills That Can Be Supported Within Content	Examples of Writing-Related Social-Emotional Skills That Can Be Supported in Modeling
• Demonstrating how to use a feelings chart to support showing feelings in a story • Demonstrating how writing can be a tool for problem-solving in the class (i.e., writing a convincing letter, making a card for someone who is missed or sad, journaling or writing stories to process a difficult moment) • Demonstrating how a related conflict can be resolved in the content of a text	• Persisting through spelling a tricky word • Taking turns with partners • Finding a just-right spot to write • Taking movement or sensory breaks • Using optimism to try something new • Using positive self-talk while writing

Chart 5.4 can be used to think about how to incorporate shared interests, experiences, and social-emotional development in the content and use of demonstration texts.

Use this tool if ... you are planning a socially-emotionally responsive demonstration text for a specific class or small group of students in mind.

Revisit this tool ... for new genre studies or when demonstrating non–genre-related writing behaviors/processes.

To use this tool, you will need ... social-emotional–related information collected about students (see Chapter 1). It is also helpful to work alongside instructional plans. Reference any demonstration text(s) included in curricular plans and/or previously created demonstration texts to modify.

Make this tool your own by ... making room to sketch/draft the demonstration text, or use the information filled out on the tool to annotate the demonstration text for instructional use and/or student use.

CHART 5.4

CONNECTING STUDENT INTERESTS, SHARED EXPERIENCES, AND SOCIAL-EMOTIONAL DEVELOPMENT TO DEMONSTRATION TEXTS

Genre Study or Area of Focus: Personal Narratives	
Current topics of shared interests and experiences: – Living in a city community – Games, sports, art, music	**Possible connections to content of a demonstration text:** – Writing about field day at school—walking to the park in the city (shared experience)
Current developing habits of mind, writing behaviors, or social-emotional skills: – Questioning or comparing oneself to peers – Beauty in diversity—connect to "diversity makes life possible" from sustainability curriculum	**Possible connections to content or modeling of a demonstration text:** – Even in competitions, we all contributed to the game, using strengths to work together – Community setup—art: face painting and T-shirt stamping; dance: dance area and DJ setup; sports: how diversity of our school community and our different choices made the day beautiful
Current developing habits of mind, writing behaviors, or social-emotional skills: – Noticing others, noticing details	**Possible connections to content or modeling of a demonstration text:** – Remembering, reflecting on, and recording details in text—details of games, emotions, art projects, DJ, and dance party

online resources 🔖 Available for download at **resources.corwin.com/responsivewritingteacher.**

Responsive Demonstration Texts Across the Domains

While this book is structured so that each domain can be returned to when focusing on any given area of responsiveness, the domains are not mutually exclusive. the following classroom example shows how academic, linguistic, cultural, and social-emotional responsiveness become integrated in instruction.

Putting It in Practice

Paul Shirk, an upper-elementary educator, shares stories of how he develops a culture of writing in the classroom:

I want students to know that writers live emotional lives.	I try to imply, early on in the school year, both the "everyday-ness" and romance of writing. I talk about all the places I write—the everyday ones, like in bed, or on the subway—and the places I escape to—beneath a tree or at my favorite coffee shop. I reference those places all year, and students begin to find their writing-in-the-world spots as well.
I wrote a piece for the *New York Times* about a racialized interaction I had with another parent. I shared the story of being so angry and how that process of writing through the anger looked. Kids were really curious about that. It was eye opening for them and made writing feel real. It gave them permission to write about times they were angry. Previously, I suspect, many of them thought that writing, especially in school, had to be about something happy. There's definitely a happiness bias in early-elementary writing workshops. I hope sharing, this demonstration opened space for a fuller range of feelings.	I applied for a fellowship of writing and talked about it in the classroom. We marked the acceptance announcement on the calendar. One kid, who I was still forming a connection with, asked about the fellowship every day. There is relationship building through vulnerability. When I didn't get accepted, it was an opportunity to explore the submission-rejection process writers face.

Digging Deeper

Throughout the chapter, we referenced specific resources. To read more about any of these concepts, we recommend the following books:

- *DIY Literacy: Teaching Tools for Differentiation, Rigor, and Independence* by Kate Roberts and Maggie Beattie Roberts (2016)

- *Inside Writing: How to Teach the Details of Craft* by Donald H. Graves and Penny Kittle (2005)

- *Every Child Can Write, Grades 2–5: Entry Points, Bridges, and Pathways for Striving Writers* by Melanie Meehan (2019)

- *Day by Day: Refining Writing Workshop Through 180 Days of Reflective Practice* by Stacey Shubitz and Ruth Ayres (2010)

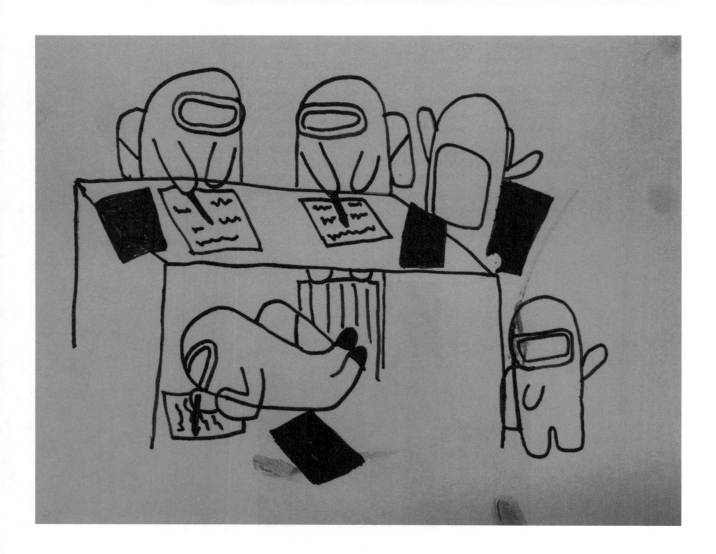

Tool for Planning Across the Domains

Demonstration Texts

This tool can be used as a place to take notes, reflect, or expand upon the ideas in this chapter. Alternatively, it can also be used to plan for responsiveness across the domains.

Academic Responsiveness	Linguistic Responsiveness
• *Models skills students are developing* • *Provides multiple entry points for developing skills*	• *Mirrors structure and length that students can produce* • *Supports new vocabulary with definitions, visuals, and/or labels*
Cultural Responsiveness	**Social-Emotional Responsiveness**
• *Portrays the identities and experiences that are familiar and unfamiliar to students*	• *Includes student interests and/or shared experiences* • *Models social-emotional skills and positive habits of mind*

CHAPTER 6

Empowering Students to Make Their Own Tools and Resources

In a Human Restoration Project *podcast, Cornelius Minor stated the following:*

> *So much of teaching has become this kind of cult of personality about the teacher. And really, it has to be about the community of kids that I'm serving. And so I'm really interested in, and again, to answer the question really specifically—of moving from this teacher monologue to authentic dialogue where we are engaging with children about crafting sustainable futures for them. (McNutt, 2019)*

> *Guiding students with self-assessing, setting goals, creating or sourcing tools, and selecting resources brings longevity to responsive instruction—equipping and sustaining students for a future in which writing is a tool for amplifying voices, solving problems, instilling change, healing, documenting, and inventing. However uncertain, such a future is one in which students learn to be the trailblazer of their own narrative.*

In planning this book, we knew no chapter would hold greater importance than this one. After all, time is limited with each group of students; a limited amount of time to nurture a love of writing, to move alongside children in their path, to celebrate and share their writing with the world.

Sure, on paper (and in many sections of this book), goals derive from developmental progressions. But reaching those expectations isn't the ultimate goal. When students leave the classroom and go off into the world, the skills, habits, mindsets, and identities they've cultivated as writers have the power to propel them to continue the work long into the future. What is built with them in the classrooms is the foundation for what can come. The most important skills are transferable—applicable in the classroom *and* in the world, as practitioners in writing workshops *and* practitioners in the world.

In the spring of 2020, students around the world left their classrooms much sooner than anticipated. A global pandemic—COVID-19—was not in curricular plans. Yet, with little time to prepare, students navigated school in unprecedented ways. This chapter, where we originally intended to tinker, explore, and dream with students as they grow agency of their learning, feels suddenly more urgent than ever.

During the time we wrote this chapter under quarantine orders, our own work in the

districts we serve has pivoted from predetermined units and genre studies to writing projects that must be immediately purposeful, relevant, and abundant with choice. We're supporting children and families with creating schedules, plans, workspaces, tools, and goals that are responsive to unique and diverse needs. During the spring of 2020, children spent more time working independently than ever before—documenting history in journals, sending mail to loved ones, hanging signs in windows, and taking their writing to the streets for protests against police brutality.

At the time of writing this chapter, we're not sure how the education system will evolve. We think of Arundhati Roy's (2020) quote: "Historically, pandemics have forced humans to break with the past and imagine their world anew. This one is no different. It is a portal, a gateway between one world and the next."

We are certain of this, however: It is imperative to teach students how to—independently, and with peers—assess, set goals, practice, and seek inspiration and mentors from in school or in the world. By doing so, preparedness shifts from developmental benchmarks and standardized tests to preparedness for self- and peer reliance. We cannot guarantee whether students will learn in our physical classroom environment, nor that they will always have educators and environments that are responsive. Because of this, the dynamic of responsiveness changes from *teacher responding to students* to *students responding to circumstance*—to problems or opportunities, to environment, to stakeholders.

This chapter culminates from all of the work presented in previous chapters. As with everything leading up to this point, we hope to inspire more than overwhelm. Throughout, you'll find charts that represent the gradual release of the components of writing instruction. Knowing that the gradual release model correlates to effective instruction and learning (Fisher & Frey, 2013), we recommend progressing along a continuum from teacher driven to student driven. There are also examples and dialogues for teaching into the processes and tools involved so that children have a clear understanding of the *why* and *how* before getting started.

Empowering students is often the messiest, most nonlinear, off-the-script teaching but also the most creative, innovative, fulfilling, and fun! We've outlined a process for student-driven work, because we're teachers, and teachers lean on outlines and processes. But this process is not definitive, and it is ever evolving. So we're inviting you into the process. Tinker, explore, dream, loosen up the reins, and *get messy*.

A Preview of This Chapter . . .

The structure mirrors the structure of the book, with a shift in focus from *responsiveness through the four domains* to *responsiveness through student-driven learning*:

- Assessments
- Planning
- Charts
- Mentor texts
- Demonstration texts

In each section, we share the following:

- *Why* student-driven learning matters
- *How* to gradually release ownership of learning through a continuum of teacher driven, to teacher facilitated, to student driven
- *What* student-driven learning can look like, in photographs, from Grades K–5.
- *What about the domains of responsiveness?*

Although we don't structure this chapter around the four domains of responsiveness in the same way as we have in other chapters, the domains are relevant and integrated here. We believe there is no greater responsiveness than student-made choices, modifications or creations of assessments, plans, charts, mentor texts, and demonstration texts. When student driven and student created, these components of writing instruction can do the following:

- Align with students' individual strengths and goals *(academic responsiveness)*
- Be written with language that students can access *(linguistic responsiveness)*
- Display text and visuals that reflect students' identities *(cultural responsiveness)*
- Incorporate students' interests and social-emotional development *(social-emotional responsiveness)*

Student-Driven Assessments

Why Do Student-Driven Assessments Matter?

A culture that habitualizes self-assessment, reflection, goal setting, and growth is one that celebrates process over product (as shared in Chapter 2). In such a classroom environment, students navigate their own learning. Self-assessment and self-selected goals are practices that are among the highest influences on student achievement (Hattie, 2017).

How Can Students Grow Ownership of Assessments?

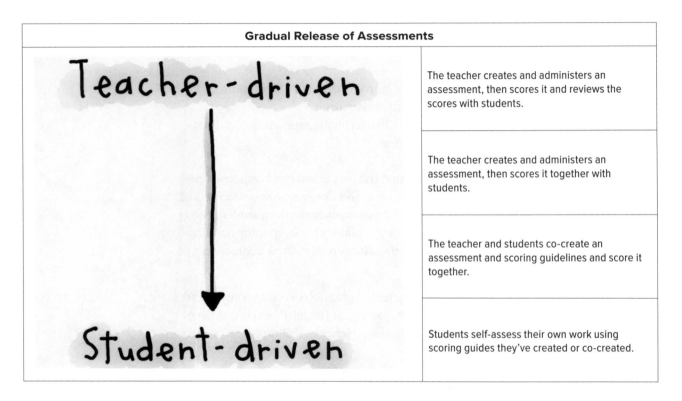

Gradual Release of Assessments	
Teacher-driven ↓ **Student-driven**	The teacher creates and administers an assessment, then scores it and reviews the scores with students.
	The teacher creates and administers an assessment, then scores it together with students.
	The teacher and students co-create an assessment and scoring guidelines and score it together.
	Students self-assess their own work using scoring guides they've created or co-created.

The tools teachers use to assess student work can be made more accessible for students by adding visuals, labels, and simplifying text. Checklists, rubrics (see Chapter 1), and progressions (see Chapter 5) can all serve as tools for self-assessment.

To introduce students to self-assessment tools, try the following steps:

1. Name the purpose of the tool. This might sound like "This tool is called a (rubric/checklist/progression), and it can help writers notice all of the things they are already doing in their writing and decide on things they can work on or add to their writing."

2. Model the following process for the class by using your own writing or alongside a student with their writing.

3. Have students read writing in their writing folder.

4. Give students their own copy of a self-assessment tool (make sure it is supported by visuals and accessible language) to look at alongside their writing.

5. Students can circle sections of the self-assessment tool that match their writing using one color.

6. Students can circle sections of the self-assessment tool that they would like to work on using a second color.

7. Each student's self-assessment tool can be saved in their writing folder to reference and track progress throughout a unit of study.

Just as students can play a role in defining expectations of writing, students can also develop awareness of their own writing process descriptions and their own processes, much like Melanie and Kelsey did in Chapter 1. Students can create their own visuals, and they can also identify their own tendencies (Berger, Rugen, & Wooden, 2014).

What Can Student-Driven Assessments Look Like?

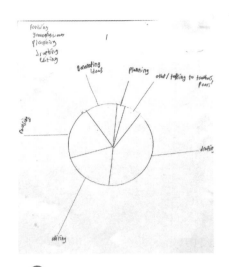

A

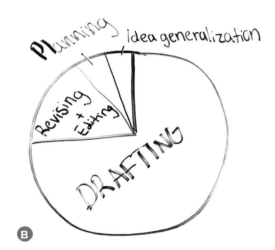

B

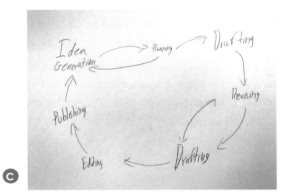

C

D

E

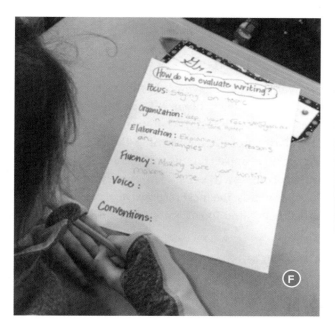

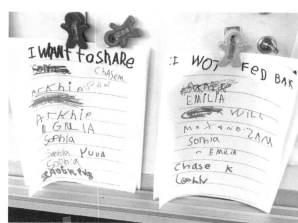

Student Reflection Form

What were the important things you learned about information writing?

What helped you learn the most?

What do you still find hard?

How could we have taught this unit differently that might have made it better for you?

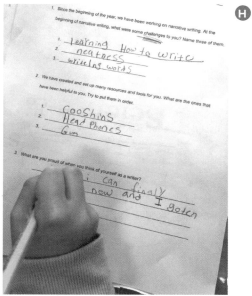

A B C These three pictures represent various students' interpretations of their own writing processes.

D Students can use the checklist to self-assess their work.

E Students can bring their writing to this area of the classroom and use sticky notes to self-reflect.

F Students help create the defining qualities of the six traits of writing as they show up on assessments: focus, organization, elaboration, fluency, voice, and conventions.

G Student Reflection Form
This student reflection form inspires students to consider their own learning in terms of what they have learned, what has helped them, and what they still could work on.

H Opportunities for reflection before, during, and after writing units help students develop their awareness of goals.

I Students sign up as they want to share their work with peers or request feedback from peers.

J Students can record hopes and dreams at the beginning of the school year or before new writing units.

Student-Driven Planning

Why Do Student-Driven Plans Matter?

Research is clear that greater motivation and achievement follow a strong sense of autonomy, competence, and relevance to learning (Ryan & Deci, 2000). Self-efficacy can also lead to higher levels of learning (Hattie, 2017). Therefore, the more students self-select their learning and have clarity around that learning, the more responsive instruction can be, having a greater positive impact on student learning. While student ownership is fostered in the selection of one's own goal, student agency develops in the planning process that follows. In other words, the most responsive plans grow from a foundation of individual and shared goals (Mind Tools Content Team, n.d.).

How Can Students Grow Ownership of Plans?

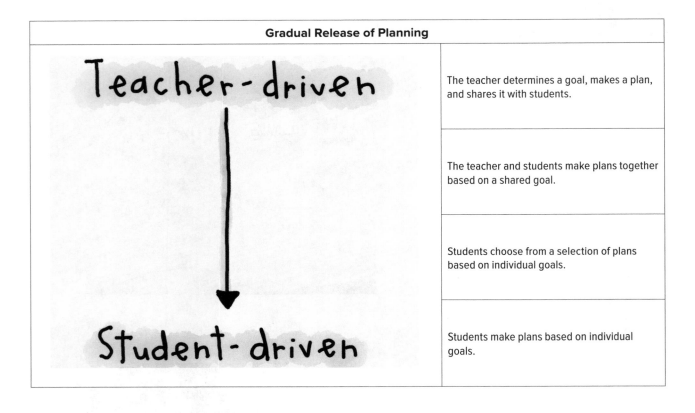

Gradual Release of Planning	
Teacher-driven ↓ Student-driven	The teacher determines a goal, makes a plan, and shares it with students.
	The teacher and students make plans together based on a shared goal.
	Students choose from a selection of plans based on individual goals.
	Students make plans based on individual goals.

Just as we set goals and plan for students after collecting information (see Chapter 2), students can be guided with setting their own goals after a self-assessment, and those goals become the differentiated plans for students (Berger et al., 2014). Goal setting increases self-confidence, motivation, and autonomy (Locke & Latham, 2006). In our experience, the goals that students set themselves, even the youngest learners, often match the goals that teachers have set for them. If a goal is too easy for a student, they may meet that goal quickly and then set a new one. If a goal is too lofty, a teacher might step in and help break that goal into some manageable steps.

There are a number of ways to support students with goal setting:

- Offer a selection of goals to choose from (the class can help generate a list of things they are working on, then select a goal from the list).
- Use a self-assessment tool so students can identify things they are doing as writers and select things to work on.
- When conferring with a student, if a student shares something they are working on or something that feels tricky, support them by naming the goal and brainstorming strategies or ways to work toward the goal.

Once students self-assess their work and set goals, we can guide them with making plans. This can be modeled with a shared goal, such as learning how to write comics, writing for a certain amount of time, or making sure noise levels don't get too loud during work time. We can say, "Plans are a tool that people make when there is something to do. Some people make plans for things to do on a playdate, some people make plans for what to do on a trip, some people make plans for what to eat during the week. We can make plans to help us (name class goal). What are some things we can do to work toward this goal?"

This process of *naming the goal* then *generating* and *narrowing ideas* into a plan can be repeated in whole-class sessions, small groups, and conferences.

What Can Student-Driven Goals and Plans Look Like?

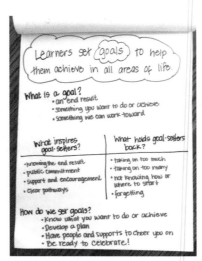

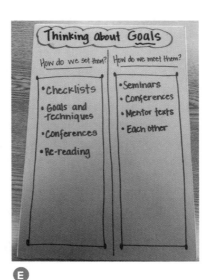

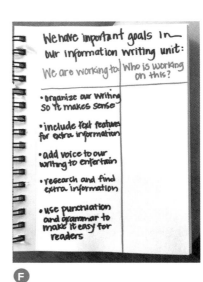

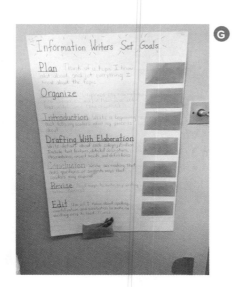

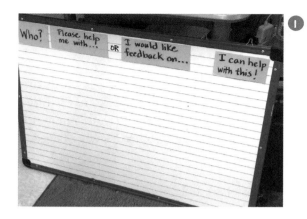

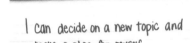

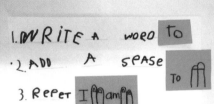

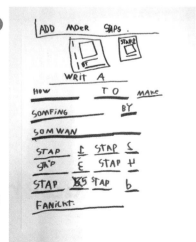

(A) Students sign up for clubs based on self-selected goals.

(B) Students reflect on "glows" and "grows" during a genre study on a folder of work they are taking home.

(C) This tool, which allows students to clarify goals that are strategies and habits, is kept in a writing folder.

(D) Students shared their ideas about goals, which were recorded on this chart.

(E) This tool, made from the ideas of students, helps with setting and meeting goals.

(F) This chart can be used with sticky notes or by adding pockets and craft sticks so that students can set and modify goals.

(G) Students selected goals from co-created options. This chart was then used to create and plan for small-group work. Students use craft sticks or cards to show what they would like to work on.

(H) A student made a plan for the day during remote instruction.

(I) Students use this board to request peer feedback and offer support.

(J) Students sign up for seminars by signing up under a larger sticky note.

(K) This chart helps students set goals within the process of research and information writing. Students determine from where in the process they were going to begin.

(L) Students attach clothespins to a table menu pocket to show goals they are working on. This tool is placed at the table where students work on that goal.

(M) This tool was created by students who set a goal to add spaces between words.

(N) A student made a plan for adding more steps to procedural texts.

Student-Driven Charts

Why Do Student-Driven Charts Matter?

In Melanie's home, there is a space that has become a temporary gym during the COVID-19 era, when there was no access to public workout facilities. Melanie's daughters, Cecily and Julia, have designed charts for the walls, reminding them to squat properly, keep breathing, and maintain their focus. "It's what I need to remember," Cecily said.

We are ever inspired by charts shared by teachers and offered in curricular guides. Rather than replicate, we've learned to re-create charts, making any modifications for responsiveness that apply to our students. By doing so, a deeper understanding of the chart leads to more effective instruction. Similarly, through moments of needing to create a chart for a unique need, we've found it immensely helpful to know the different kinds of charts and purposes they serve, as shared in Chapter 3.

The charts that are created and shared with a class may be just right for many students. But by taking students through the process of chart creation, we can then provide copies for students to make modifications that match their needs and goals. Finally, it's possible to provide templates and materials for students to make their own charts. These practices equip students to seek out, utilize, and create charts that provide support for any goal at any time.

How Can Students Grow Ownership of Charts?

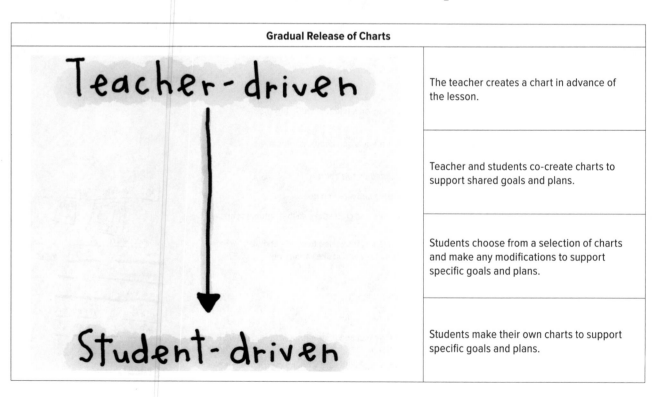

Gradual Release of Charts	
Teacher-driven ↓ Student-driven	The teacher creates a chart in advance of the lesson.
	Teacher and students co-create charts to support shared goals and plans.
	Students choose from a selection of charts and make any modifications to support specific goals and plans.
	Students make their own charts to support specific goals and plans.

When co-creating charts with students, we can say that charts are tools that are helpful for following plans and working toward goals. It can be powerful to link co-created charts to any shared goals and plans.

We can say, "Some kinds of charts show *what something needs to have.* Teachers call these *anchor charts,* and they can look like this (show example). Some kinds of charts show *how to do something*, and they can look like this (show example). Teachers call these *process charts.* Some kinds of charts show *different ways to do something*. Teachers call these *strategy charts,* and they can look like this (show example). For our goal (name goal), we need to know (what _____ needs to have / how to _____ / different ways to _____) so we can make a (name kind of chart). Let's try that together now."

- Anchor charts help to answer "What do I need to do?"
- Process charts help to answer "How do I do this?"
- Strategy charts help to answer "What are some ways I can do this?"

We can guide students through this process again and again, as different shared needs and purposes arise and can be supported by different kinds of charts.

- Throughout a genre study, and across the year, photocopies of charts can be kept at a student writing center. Students can select charts that match specific goals or as needed.
- By providing sticky notes and markers, we can model and coach students to make changes or add on to charts.
- Students can share revised charts with the class, demonstrating how to make charts match individual goals and needs.
- Tools such as blank paper or cardstock, scissors, hole punchers, sticky notes, glue sticks, tape, and markers can be kept in the writing center for student-made charts (as well as for a variety of purposes named and modeled throughout the year).
- In a goal-setting conference or small-group planning session, we can support students with creating their own charts, making sure to name the purpose: Will the chart show *what something should have, how to do something,* or *different ways to do something*?

What Can Student-Driven Charts Look Like?

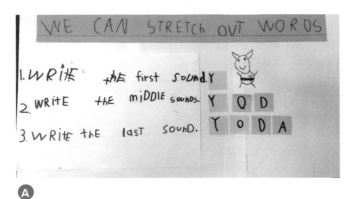

A

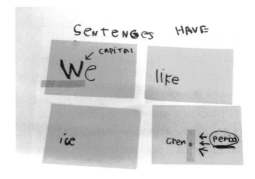

B

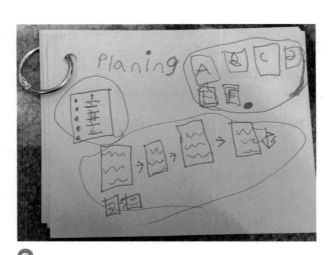

C

D

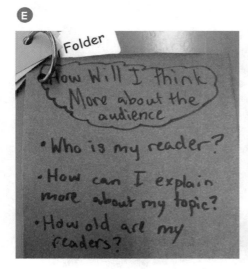

E

F

G

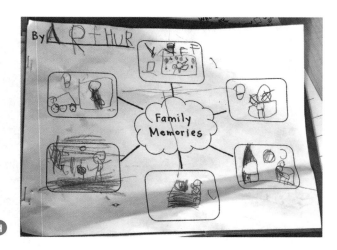

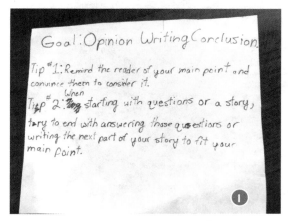

A Students make a chart to show how to stretch through sounds in a word.

B Students make this tool to remind themselves of sentence conventions.

C A student draws pictures as a reminder of options for planning an information piece.

D This student incorporates their own elements of design for this strategy chart.

E This student keeps self-selected reminders on a ring.

F A student makes a personal resource for remembering the features and processes of narrative writing.

G This strategy chart reminds a student how to elaborate in information writing.

H Students use a tool made with photos and drawings as a reminder of memories for idea generation.

I J K These students reflect on self-talk from a fixed mindset to a growth mindset.

L Students add pictures and self-talk for traits of a growth mindset.

M

N

O

P

Q

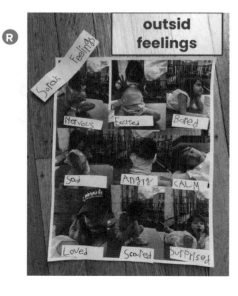

R

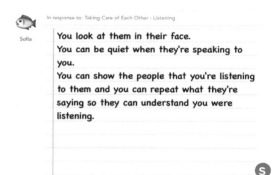

Sofia

In response to: Taking Care of Each Other - Listening

You look at them in their face.
You can be quiet when they're speaking to you.
You can show the people that you're listening to them and you can repeat what they're saying so they can understand you were listening.

S

Thu, May 14, 2020

HA
Hayes

In response to: What can you do with big feelings?

Calm myself, big deep breath
Sigh
Hug my mom
Cry
Bounce around the house

T

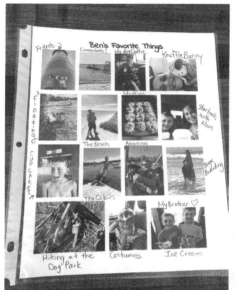

U

V

W

X

M Students can select their own tools from this classroom area.

N Students contribute shared interests and experiences in this class idea book.

O A student creates a word wall at home to reference when writing.

P A student creates a reminder for optimism.

Q R Students create their own feelings charts to keep at home and upload photos of them on Seesaw.

S T Students use Seesaw to create strategy charts for listening (left) and navigating big feelings (right).

U Students make charts of things they enjoy to serve as an idea-generation tool.

V W Students plan just-right writing spots.

X Students make a vowel chart.

Student-Driven Mentor Texts

Why Do Student-Driven Mentor Texts Matter?

When incorporating mentor authors and texts throughout the year (as shared in Chapter 4)—beyond noticing *what* authors and illustrators of particular genres do—we can show *how* writers are inspired by other writers and texts. Then, students begin reading as writers, devouring the classroom library, requesting to write alongside their favorites. The mentor texts students often study with the most care, the ones that students have requested to house in writing folders, the ones that they have returned to day after day are the ones they have selected themselves.

How Can Students Grow Ownership of Mentor Texts?

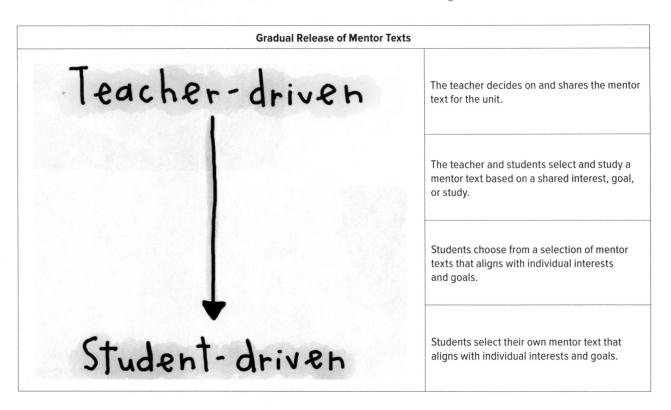

Gradual Release of Mentor Texts	
Teacher-driven ↓ Student-driven	The teacher decides on and shares the mentor text for the unit.
	The teacher and students select and study a mentor text based on a shared interest, goal, or study.
	Students choose from a selection of mentor texts that aligns with individual interests and goals.
	Students select their own mentor text that aligns with individual interests and goals.

When introducing a mentor text to students, name the purpose by saying, "Sometimes people see something that gives them new ideas, or see someone that shows them how to do something. They get inspired, which means they want to try it too. Maybe that's happened to you before—when you saw a friend or family member do something, when you saw something on TV or in a video, maybe a musician or athlete. Think about a time when you've been inspired, or wanted to try something you saw before. Then (turn and tell a partner/sketch/make a movie in your mind/choose how to share) about it."

Another way to introduce mentor texts and authors might be this: "Something special happens to writers when they read. They can get inspired too. Writers are inspired by authors and illustrators when they can show us how to do something. Writers are inspired by books when they give us new ideas. There's a special word people use for someone or something that inspires them: *mentor.* Try saying it with me, *mentor.*"

From here, and throughout the year, there are several ways to foster ownership and agency as this process unfolds—gradually releasing the process of using mentor texts as a tool:

- The teacher can unveil a mentor text or author/illustrator that students are familiar with, then students name text elements and craft moves that inspire them, as the teacher names, annotates, and/or records these.
- Students can vote on a mentor to study from several familiar related read alouds.
- Copies of annotated pages from a mentor text can be available at the writing center, so students can choose to study parts that align with needs and goals.
- Several mentor texts can be studied throughout a genre study, and students can choose which mentor text they reference.
- The teacher can curate, or co-curate with students, a bin of genre-specific texts. Students are given time to explore the bin of books (at once, if there are enough, or at different times . . . and individually or with a partner), then select one to study during independent writing time.
- Students may find their own mentor text in the library, at home, or digitally and request to use it at writing time.

What Can Student-Driven Mentor Texts Look Like?

In Chapter 4, we emphasized the importance of having a collection of representative mentor texts for students to choose from. Having a self-help shelf where students can choose a book to use as a mentor and refer to the chart of craft moves within the book encourages the use of books as teachers. In a guest post on the *Two Writing Teachers* blog, Meghan Hargrave (2020) writes about the "silent teachers" in a writing classroom, describing them as "all the things in the classroom that help (students) write, *besides* an adult." Mentor texts are these sorts of resources.

(A)

(B)

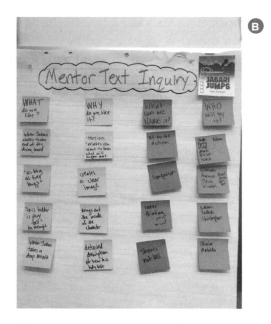

(C)

(D)

(E)

(F)

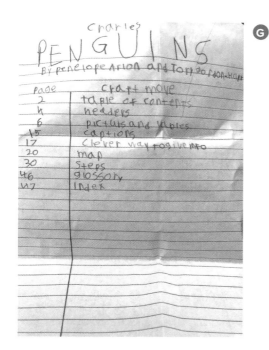

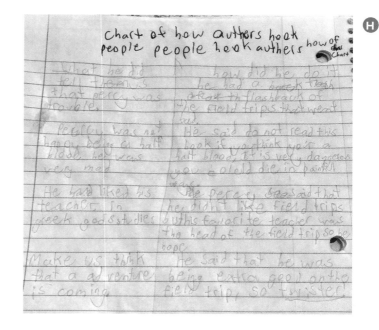

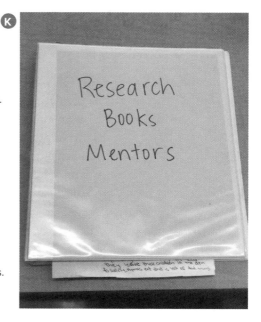

A Student mentor texts are annotated in this chart and added to the mentor text selection bin.

B This guided mentor text inquiry incorporates student-driven plans.

C This tool supports children with selecting and using a mentor text.

D Students name ways to hook readers through a guided inquiry of several mentor texts.

E This chart, developed over time, names craft moves. Students print and highlight portions of their own writing that demonstrates the elaboration strategies they found in books they admired.

F G In these two examples, students list page numbers and craft moves they found in a narrative and a nonfiction text.

H This student researches ways mentors have hooked readers.

I Students in small groups study the ways a mentor shows feelings. They chart their noticings.

J K Students can choose from a collection of student or published mentor texts, each annotated to highlight specific elements and craft moves.

Student-Driven Demonstration Texts

Why Do Student-Driven Demonstration Texts Matter?

Not only are demonstration texts an effective tool for modeling specific skills, the process of creating them leads to a deeper understanding of the process involved with such skills. Students can be involved in this process of thinking specifically and explicitly about how to practice a certain skill—then create a model of that skill for themselves or others. As the Chinese proverb reminds us, "Tell me and I'll forget; show me and I may remember; involve me and I'll understand."

How Can Students Grow Ownership of Demonstration Texts?

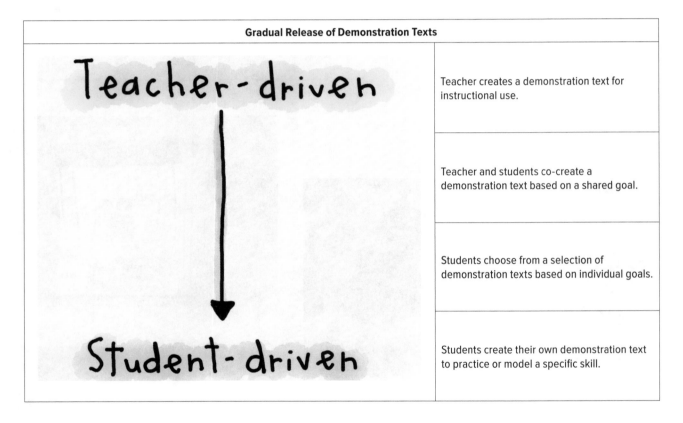

Gradual Release of Demonstration Texts	
Teacher-driven ↓ Student-driven	Teacher creates a demonstration text for instructional use.
	Teacher and students co-create a demonstration text based on a shared goal.
	Students choose from a selection of demonstration texts based on individual goals.
	Students create their own demonstration text to practice or model a specific skill.

Involving students in the creation and modeling of a demonstration text can happen at any point. For an especially powerful progression of the learning process, this can occur after any combination of the following: a shared class goal is made, a plan has been drafted for working on that goal, a chart has been co-created to support that goal, and a mentor text has been studied that models that goal. Now, students can practice that goal in a demonstration text.

There are a number of options for selecting a text to use for a student-driven demonstration. No matter the source of the text, it should be one that has room for practicing the specific skill or goal. It's helpful if students are already familiar with the content of the text. If it is the first time they are introduced to it, read it first before using it to model. The following texts can all become demonstration texts:

- A previously cowritten text (Because all students were involved in its creation through shared writing or interactive writing, this option is most recommended.)
- A student's text (used with permission) is also effective and a source for enlarging the work
- A text that has been prewritten by the teacher

We can invite students in on the process of using a demonstration text by saying, "We've been doing lots of work to help us with the goal of (name goal). I brought some of the tools we've used so far. One thing—one of the most important things, I should say—people do when they are working on a goal is . . . practice! So I thought we could do that right now. What better way to practice than by writing?"

At this point, instead of directly modeling the skill for students, we can guide them with deliberate practice of the skill, gradually releasing ownership. This can happen several ways, in large or small groups, in multiple sessions:

- The teacher first models what students are working on at one part of the text, using co-created tools to support. Then, students look for more places in the text to practice and use tools. Teachers share the pen to allow students to model for the class. To actively engage as many students as possible in this, do the following:
  - Invite students to turn and talk about how they would revise or edit the piece based on the focus.
  - Distribute photocopies, and invite students or partnerships to practice directly on the text.
- Once multiple pages of a demonstration text have been annotated with revisions or edits, or once several demonstration texts have been used, add copies to the writing center. Invite students to reference demonstration texts that match their individual needs and goals.
- Finally, if students are working on their own goals individually or in a small group, they can demonstrate using their own work for the class during a share or teach session. Annotated photocopies of their work can be added to tools in the writing center.

What Can Student-Driven Demonstration Texts Look Like?

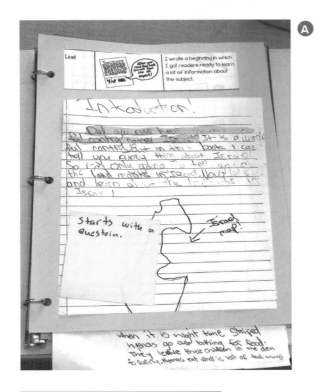

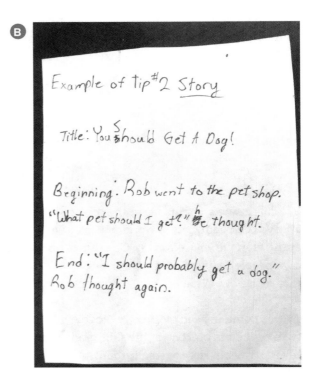

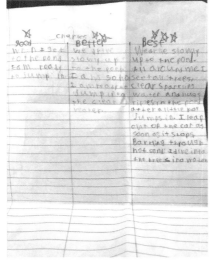

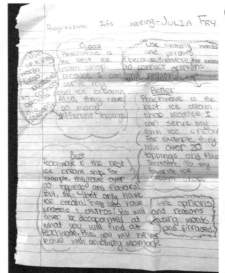

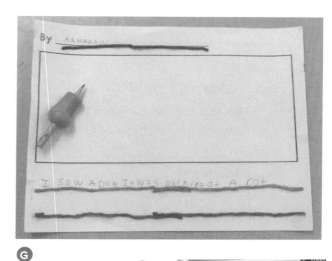

Interview with June the gardner

A A student annotates their own text to demonstrate a lead in an introduction.

B A student creates a demonstration text to remember how to use an engaging story at the beginning and end of an information piece to hook readers.

C A student creates a progression to show the development of the beginning of a personal narrative.

D A student records notes and reminders for writing strong introductions in opinion writing.

E A student creates a text to demonstrate spaces between words.

F A student uses a highlighter during oral rehearsal to reinforce concepts of print.

G A student uses wax craft sticks for a tactile demonstration of print awareness on writing paper.

H A student uses a different colored writing utensil to demonstrate labeling illustrations.

I A student demonstrates the recording of an interview by using different colors to show the structure of questions and answers.

J K Students demonstrate craft moves made in their writing.

Tool for Planning

Student-Driven Work

This tool can be used as a place to take notes, reflect, or expand upon the ideas in this chapter. Alternatively, it can also be used to plan for student-driven work.

Assessments	Planning
Charts	**Mentor Texts**
Demonstration Texts	**Other**

Bibliography
and References

Ahmed, R. (2018). *Mae among the stars*. New York, NY: HarperCollins.

Ahmed, S. (2018). *Being the change. Lessons and strategies to teach social comprehension*. Portsmouth, NH: Heinemann.

Alexander, K. (2019). *How to read a book*. New York, NY: HarperCollins.

American Speech-Language-Hearing Association. (n.d.). What is speech? What is language. Retrieved from www.asha.org/public/speech/development/language_speech/

Anderson, C. (2018). *A teacher's guide to writing conferences*. Portsmouth, NH: Heinemann.

Baker-Bell, A. (2020). *Linguistic justice: Black language, literacy, identity, and pedagogy*. New York, NY: Routledge.

Bandura, A. (1977). Self-efficacy: Toward a unifying theory of behavioral change. *Psychological Review, 84*, 191–215.

Berger, R., Rugen, L., & Wooden, L. (2014). *Leaders of their own learning: Transforming schools through student-engaged assessment*. San Francisco, CA: Jossey-Bass.

Boelts, M. (2016). *A bike like Sergio's*. Somerville, MA: Candlewick.

Calkins, L. M. (2008). *The art of teaching writing*. Portsmouth, NH: Heinemann. (Original work published 1986)

Cherry-Paul, S. (2019). *Meaningful inquiry by taking stock of self, school, and book characters*. Paper presented at the NCTE Annual Convention, Baltimore, MD.

Cherry-Paul, S., & Johansen, D. (2019). *Building better readers through book clubs!* Paper presented at the NCTE Annual Convention, Baltimore, MD.

Cooperative Children's Book Center. (2020, June 16). The numbers are in: 2019 CCBC diversity statistics. Retrieved from http://ccblogc.blogspot.com/2020/06/the-numbers-are-in-2019-ccbc-diversity.html

Cornwall, G. (2020). *Jabari jumps*. Somerville, MA: Candlewick Press.

Crenshaw, K.(1989), Demarginalizing the intersection of race and sex: A black feminist critique of antidiscrimination doctrine, feminist theory and antiracist politics," *University of Chicago Legal Forum, 1989*, 8. Retrieved from: https://chicagounbound.uchicago.edu/uclf/vol1989/iss1/8

Dorfman, L. R., & Cappelli, R. (2017). *Mentor texts: Teaching writing through children's literature, K–6* (2nd ed.). Portsmouth, NH: Stenhouse Publishers.

Duyvis, C. (2015). #Ownvoices. Retrieved from https://www.corinneduyvis.net/ownvoices/

Dweck, C. S. (2006). *Mindset: The new psychology of success*. New York, NY: Random House.

Eakins, S. (2020). Episode #142: Making noise about the things that matter with Kelisa Wing [Podcast transcript]. Retrieved from https://www.leadingequitycenter.com/142%20transcript

Eakins. S. (2020, July 20). Episode #148: A discussion on linguistic equity with Dr. Barbara (BK) Kennedy [Podcast transcript]. Retrieved from https://www.leadingequitycenter.com/148

Eickholdt, L. (2015). *Learning from classmates: Using students' writing as mentor texts.* Portsmouth, NH: Heinemann.

Elliott, Z. (2019). *The dragon thief.* New York, NY: Random House Children's Books.

Everett, C. (2017, November 21). There is no diverse book. Retrieved from http://www.imaginelit.com/news/2017/11/21/there-is-no-diverse-book

Everett, C. (2018, November 25). Beyond our shelves. Retrieved from http://www.imaginelit.com/news?offset=1556964000955

Facing History and Ourselves. (n.d.). Identity charts. Retrieved from www.facinghistory.org/resource-library/teaching-strategies/identity-charts

Fillmore, L. W., & Snow, C. E. (2000, August 23). What teachers need to know about language. Paper prepared with funding from the U.S. Department of Education's Office of Educational Research and Improvement, under contract no. ED-99-CO-0008 to the Center for Applied Linguistics. Retrieved from https://files.eric.ed.gov/fulltext/ED444379.pdf

Fisher, D., & Frey, N. (2013). *Better learning through structured teaching: A framework for the gradual release of responsibility* (2nd ed.). Alexandria, VA: ASCD.

Fisher, D., Frey, N., & Akhavan, N. (2019). *This is balanced literacy, Grades K–6.* Thousand Oaks, CA: Corwin.

Flett, J. (2019). *Birdsong.* Vancouver, BC, Canada: Greystone Kids.

Formative Assessment for Students and Teachers (FAST) State Collaborative on Assessment and Student Standards (SCASS). (2020, October 21). Revising the definition of formative assessment. Washington, DC: Council of Chief State School Officers. Retrieved from https://ccsso.org/sites/default/files/2018-06/Revising%20the%20Definition%20of%20Formative%20Assessment.pdf

Fraser, S., & Gestwicki, C. (2012). *Authentic childhood: Experiencing Reggio Emilia in the classroom.* Belmont, CA: Wadsworth Publishing.

Frazin, S., & Wischow, K. (2019). *Unlocking the power of classroom talk: Teaching kids to talk with clarity and purpose.* Portsmouth, NH: Heinemann.

Giovanni, N. (2008). *Hip hop speaks to children: A celebration of poetry with a beat.* Naperville, IL: Sourcebooks eXplore.

Goldenberg, C. (2008, Summer). Teaching English language learners: What the research does—and does not—say. *American Educator.* Retrieved from https://www.aft.org/sites/default/files/periodicals/goldenberg.pdf

Goodman, Y. M. (1985). Kidwatching: Observing children in the classroom. In A. Jagger & M. T. Smith-Burke (Eds.), *Observing the language learner* (pp. 9–18). Urbana, IL: NCTE and IRA.

Graham, S., & Harris, K. R. (2016, January 5). A path to better writing: Evidence-based practices in the classroom. *The Reading Teacher, 69,* 359–365.

Graves, D. H. (1983). *Writing: Teachers and children at work.* Portsmouth, NH: Heinemann.

Graves, D. H. (2020). All children can write. Retrieved from http://www.ldonline.org/article/6204 (Original work published 1985)

Graves, D. H., & Kittle, P. (2005). *Inside writing: How to teach the details of craft.* Portsmouth, NH: Heinemann.

Hamid, R. (2017). *Kadisa* كديسة *: A journey through Sudan.* Author.

Hammond, Z. (2015). Culturally responsive teaching and the brain: Promoting authentic engagement and rigor among culturally and linguistically diverse students. Thousand Oaks, CA: Corwin.

Hargrave, M. (2020, February 26). The power of silent teachers: Helping writers increase productivity and build independence through interdependence with tools in the classroom [Blog post]. Retrieved from https://twowritingteachers. org/2020/02/26/hargrave/

Hattie, J. (2012). *Visible learning for teachers: Maximizing impact on learning.* New York, NY: Routledge.

Hattie, J. (2017, November). Visible Learning[plus] 250+ influences on student achievement. Retrieved from https://visible-learning.org/wp-content/uploads/2018/03/ VLPLUS-252-Influences-Hattie-ranking-DEC-2017.pdf

Heard, G. (2016). *Heart maps: Helping students create and craft authentic writing.* Portsmouth, NH: Heinemann.

Hernton, C. C. (n.d.). The distant drum. Retrieved from https://ineedtoreadmorepoetry. tumblr.com/post/126348820119/the-distant-drum-by-calvin-c-hernton

Hill, J. D., & Björk, C. L. (2008). *Classroom instruction that works with English language learners: Facilitator's guide.* Alexandria, VA: ASCD.

Horton, M., & Freire, P. (1990). *We make the road by walking: Conversations on education and social change.* Philadelphia, PA: Temple University Press.

Indiegogo. (n.d.). *Kadisa* كديسة : *A picture book about Sudan.* Retrieved from https:// www.indiegogo.com/projects/kadisa-a-picture-book-about-sudan#/

Jenkins, S. (2010). *Bones: Skeletons and how they work.* New York, NY: Scholastic Reference.

Jewell, T. (2020). *This book is anti-racist: 20 lessons on how to wake up, take action, and do the work.* London, England: Frances Lincoln Children's Books.

Keene, E. O. (2018). *Engaging children: Igniting a drive for deeper learning.* Portsmouth, NH: Heinemann.

Knight, J. (2018, May 29). An interview with Zaretta Hammond. Retrieved from https://instructionalcoaching.com/an-interview-with-zaretta-hammond/

Krashen, S. D., & Terrell, T. D. (1983). The natural approach: Language acquisition in the classroom. Hayward, CA: Alemany Press.

Krashen, S. D., & Terrell, T. D. (2000). The natural approach: Language acquisition in the classroom (Rev. ed.). New York, NY: Pearson.

Ladson-Billings, G. (1995, Summer). But that's just good teaching! The case for culturally relevant pedagogy. *Theory Into Practice, 34,* 159–165.

Laws, M. (2020, June 16). Why we capitalize "Black" (and not "white"). *Columbia Journalism Review.* Retrieved from https://www.cjr.org/analysis/capital-b-black-styleguide.php

Lewis, J., Aydin, A., & Powell, N. (2016). *March: Book one.* Marietta, GA: Top Shelf Productions.

Locke, E. A., & Latham, G. P. (2006). New directions in goal-setting theory. *Current Directions in Psychological Science, 15,* 265–268.

Lyon, G. E. (n.d.). Where I'm from. Retrieved from http://teacher.scholastic.com/write-it/PDF/lyon.pdf

Mahnke, K. (1985). The natural approach: Language acquisition in the classroom, Stephen D. Krashen and Tracy D. Terrell. Oxford: Pergamon Press, 1983. pp. vi + 191. Studies in Second Language Acquisition, 7, 364–365. doi:10.1017/s0272263100005659

Mallard, K. N. (2019). *Fry bread: A Native American family story*. New York, NY: Roaring Brook Press.

Martinelli, M., & Mraz, K. (2012). *Smarter charts K–2: Optimizing an instructional staple to create independent readers and writers*. Portsmouth, NH: Heinemann.

McMillan, J. H., & Hearn, J. (2008). Student self-assessment: The key to stronger student motivation and higher achievement. *Educational Horizons, 87*, 40–49. Retrieved from https://www.jstor.org/stable/42923742

McNutt, C. (Executive director). (2019, July 6). We got this: Equity and access in schools with Cornelius Minor [Audio podcast]. Retrieved from https://www.humanrestorationproject.org/season-3-episode-9-cornelius-minor

Meehan, M. (2019). *Every child can write, Grades 2–5: Entry points, bridges, and pathways for striving writers*. Thousand Oaks, CA: Corwin.

Méndez, Y. S. (2019). *Where are you from?* New York, NY: HarperCollins.

Mind Tools Content Team. (n.d.). Personal goal setting: Planning to live your life your way. Retrieved from https://www.mindtools.com/page6.html

Minor, C. (2018). *We got this: Equity, access, and the quest to be who our students need us to be*. Portsmouth, NH: Heinemann.

Mraz, K., & Hertz, C. (2015). *A mindset for learning: Teaching the traits of joyful, independent growth*. Portsmouth, NH: Heinemann.

National Equity Project [NEP]. (n.d.). National Equity Project definition of educational equity. Retrieved from https://www.nationalequityproject.org/education-equity-definition

Owocki, G., & Goodman, Y. (2002). Kidwatching: Documenting children's literacy development. Portsmouth, NH: Heinemann.

Parrott, K. (2018, March 7). A diversity & cultural literacy toolkit. Retrieved from https://www.slj.com/?detailStory=diversity-cultural-literacy-toolkit

Phi, B. (2017). *A different pond*. Mankato, MN: Capstone Young Readers.

Quay, L., & Romero, C. (2015, July). What we know about learning mindsets from scientific research. Retrieved form http://mindsetscholarsnetwork.org/wpcontent/uploads/2015/09/What-We-Know-About-Learning-Mindsets.pdf

Raschka, C. (2007). *Yo! Yes?* New York, NY: Orchard Paperbacks.

Ray, K. W. (2002). *What you know by heart: How to develop curriculum for your writing workshop*. Portsmouth, NH: Heinemann.

Ray, K. W. (2010). *In pictures and in words: Teaching the qualities of good writing through illustration study*. Portsmouth, NH: Heinemann.

Roberts, K., & Roberts, M. B. (2016). *DIY literacy: Teaching tools for differentiation, rigor, and independence*. Portsmouth, NH: Heinemann.

Robertson, K., & Ford, K. (2008). Language acquisition: An overview. Retrieved from http://www.ldonline.org/article/26751/

Roy, A. (2020, April 3). Arundhati Roy: "The pandemic is a portal." *Financial Times*. Retrieved from https://www.ft.com/content/10d8f5e8-74eb-11ea-95fe-fcd274e920ca

Ryan, R. M., & Deci, E. L. (2000). When rewards compete with nature: The undermining of intrinsic motivation and self-regulation. In C. Sansone & J. M. Harackiewicz (Eds.), Intrinsic and extrinsic motivation: The search for optimal motivation and performance (pp. 13–54). Cambridge, MA: Academic Press. Retrieved from https://doi.org/10.1016/B978-012619070-0/50024-6

Sagor, R. D. (2011). *The action research guidebook: A four-stage process for educators and school teams* (2nd ed.). Thousand Oaks, CA: Corwin.

Serravallo, J. (2017). *Writing strategies*. Portsmouth, NH: Heinemann.

Shubitz, S. (2016). *Craft moves: Lesson sets for teaching writing with mentor texts.* Portland, ME: Stenhouse Publishers.

Shubitz, S., & Ayres, R. (2010). *Day by day: Refining writing workshop through 180 days of reflective practice.* Portland, ME: Stenhouse Publishers.

Sims Bishop, R. (1990). Mirrors, windows, and sliding glass doors. *Perspectives: Choosing and Using Books for the Classroom, 6.*

Smith, N. (2016). *The golden girls of Rio.* New York, NY: Sky Pony.

Sousa, D. A., & Tomlinson, C. A. (2018). *Differentiation and the brain: How neuroscience supports the learner-friendly classroom* (2nd ed.). Bloomington, IN: Solution Tree Press.

Steptoe, J. (Illustrator). (2013). *In daddy's arms I am tall: African Americans celebrating fathers.* New York, NY: Lee & Low Books.

Style, E. (1988). *Listening for all voices* [Monograph]. Summit, NJ: Oak Knoll School.

Supovitz, J. (2012). Getting at student understanding—the key to teachers' use of test data. *Teachers College Record, 114,* 1–29.

Talbott, H. (2012). *It's all about me-ow.* New York, NY: Nancy Paulsen Books.

Trumbull, E., & Lash, A. (2013, April). *Understanding formative assessment: Insights from learning theory and measurement theory.* San Francisco, CA: WestEd.

Velasquez, E. (2016). *Looking for Bongo.* New York, NY: Holiday House.

Vygotsky, L. S. (1978). *Mind in society: The development of higher psychological processes.* Cambridge, MA: Harvard University Press.

Wade, R. C. (2007). *Social studies for social justice: Teaching strategies for the elementary classroom.* New York, NY: Teachers College Press.

Wiggins, G., & McTighe, J. (2011). *The Understanding by Design guide to creating high-quality units.* Alexandria, VA: ASCD.

Woodson, J. (2014). February 12, 1963. In *Brown girl dreaming.* London, England: Penguin Books.

Wright, J. T., & Hoonan, B. T. (2018). What are you grouping for? Grades 3–8: How to guide small groups based on readers—not the book. Thousand Oaks, CA: Corwin.

Wright, R. (2018). *Seeing into tomorrow.* Minneapolis, MN: Millbrook Press.

Zhang, K. (2019). *Amy Wu and the perfect bao.* New York, NY: Aladdin.

Index

Because...
ALL TEACHERS ARE LEADERS

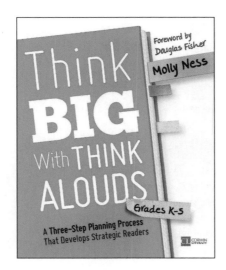

MOLLY NESS

Molly's three-step planning process will help you create dynamic lessons that focus on the five most important think aloud strategies.

DOUGLAS FISHER, NANCY FREY, AND NANCY AKHAVAN

Evidence-based approaches ensure that the teachers have all they need to achieve balance in their literacy classrooms across a wide range of critical skills.

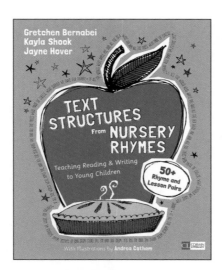

GRETCHEN BERNABEI, KAYLA SHOOK, AND JAYNE HOVER

In 53 lessons centered around classic nursery rhymes, this groundbreaking book offers a straightforward framework for guiding young children in their earliest writing efforts.

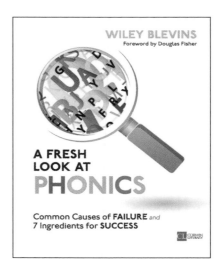

WILEY BLEVINS

Foremost phonics expert Wiley Blevins explains the 7 ingredients that lead to the greatest student gains. This resource includes common pitfalls, lessons, word lists, and routines.

To order your copies, visit corwin.com/literacy

At Corwin Literacy we have put together a collection of just-in-time, classroom-tested, practical resources from trusted experts that allow you to quickly find the information you need when you need it.

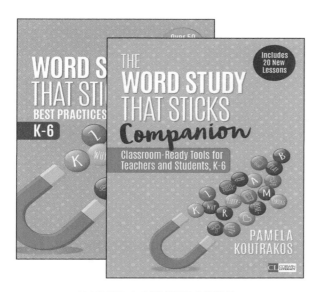

PAMELA KOUTRAKOS

Word Study That Sticks and its resource companion deliver challenging, discovery-based word learning routines and planning frameworks you can implement across subject areas.

MARIA WALTHER

101 picture-book experiences, a thousand ways to savor strategically. This is the book that shows how to use ANY book to teach readers and writers.

DOUGLAS FISHER, NANCY FREY, AND JOHN HATTIE

Ensure students demonstrate more than a year's worth of learning during a school year by implementing the right literacy practice at the right moment.

DOUGLAS FISHER, NANCY FREY, AND JOHN HATTIE

High-impact strategies to use for all you teach— all in one place. Deliver sustained, comprehensive literacy experiences to K–5 learners each day.

CORWIN

A SAGE Publishing Company

Helping educators make the greatest impact

CORWIN HAS ONE MISSION: to enhance education through intentional professional learning.

We build long-term relationships with our authors, educators, clients, and associations who partner with us to develop and continuously improve the best evidence-based practices that establish and support lifelong learning.